Making the Most of Your
Flex-shaft

Sponsor Acknowledgments

MJSA/AJM Press and The Ganoksin Project would like to thank the following companies for their sponsorship of this book.

PRIME SPONSOR
Rio Grande

PATRON
The Foredom Electric Co.

PATRON
3M Inc.

Orchid in Print: Maximum Bench Work, Volume 1

Making the Most of Your
Flex-shaft

by Karen Christians

MJSA/AJM Press
A Division of Manufacturing Jewelers & Suppliers of America

This book is dedicated to my husband, Dave, who is the wind at my back

© 2005 MJSA/AJM Press and The Ganoksin Project
ISBN 0-9713495-6-8
Library of Congress Control Number 2 005 910041

All rights reserved. No part of this book may be reproduced in any form or by any electronic or mechanical means, including information storage and retrieval systems, without permission in writing from the copyright holders, except for brief passages quoted in review. Book design by Jacki Silvan, Think Tank Creative, Alexandria, VA.

Cover photos by Gary Dawson, Goldworks, Eugene, OR.

Safety Notice: The content of this book is solely the work of the author and has not been tested or authorized by Manufacturing Jewelers & Suppliers of America, AJM Magazine, or MJSA/AJM Press. The use or application of information, practices, and/or techniques pertaining to jewelry manufacturing, jewelry repair, or other related topics in this book may be hazardous to persons and property, and they are undertaken at the reader's own risk.

Trademark Notice: The capitalization of product names indicates those names are registered trademarks. They include: 3M™ EXL wheels, 3M™ Flexible Diamond abrasives, 3M™ Mico-finishing Film, 3M™ Purple Ceramic bands and discs, 3M™ Scotch-Brite™ Radial Bristle Discs, 3M™ Trizact™ abrasive, 3M™ Unitized Wheel, 3M™ Wetordry™ Polishing Papers, AllSet® Setting System, Jacobs® Chuck handpiece.

Some of this text originally appeared, in modified form, in *AJM* Magazine, a monthly publication of Manufacturing Jewelers & Suppliers of America, or on The Ganoksin Project Web site. For information about subscribing to AJM, call 1-888-438-6572 (U.S. and Canada only) or 1-401-274-3840, or visit *AJM Online* at *www.ajm-magazine.com*. For more information about The Ganoksin Project, go to *www.ganoksin.com*.

Orchid in Print is an imprint of MJSA/AJM Press,
45 Royal Little Drive, Providence, RI 02904;
1-800-444-6572 or 1-401-274-3840; fax 1-401-274-0265;
e-mail *mjsa@mjsainc.com*; Web site *www.mjsainc.com*.

Table of Contents

Sponsor Acknowledgments	2
Author's Acknowledgments	6
Foreword	7
Chapter One: An Introduction to the Flex-shaft System	9
Chapter Two: Choosing the Proper Motor & Power Control	15
Chapter Three: Choosing the Proper Handpiece	21
Chapter Four: Choosing the Proper Bur or Drill Bit	27
Chapter Five: Choosing a Mandrel	41
Chapter Six: Abrasives & Grinding Wheels	45
Chapter Seven: Brushes, Buffs, & Polishing Compounds	57
Chapter Eight: Attachments for Your Flex-shaft	63
Chapter Nine: Maintenance & Safety Procedures	67
Chapter Ten: Beyond the Basics	68
Jewelers' Resources	79
Index	94
About the Author	96

Author's Acknowledgments

When you begin to make jewelry, there is a learning curve. First you move slowly; your hands are unsteady, and you train yourself in how to hold oddly shaped files and a saw frame. Soon your confidence builds, and you work faster. Writing is not much different. Describing technical parts and processes was, for me, like writing for a blind person that could feel and hear, but not see. Pictures developed in my mind, and the words flowed easier. However, it takes an editor to bring these written pictures to their full visual impact. Therefore, my thanks first and foremost is to my editor, Rich Youmans. Rich, you guided me through the labyrinthine process of becoming an author, and together we made an important book—the first in a series of contributions from Orchid and MJSA.

A very special thanks goes to the prime sponsor of this first edition, Rio Grande, and the patrons, Foredom Electric Co. and 3M Inc. Without your support, this important book would not have been written. In particular, I'd like to express my gratitude to Diana Montoya and Kyle of Rio Grande, Rich Bohr of 3M, and Bill Nelson and Mike Zagielski of Foredom. I also thank all of the companies that provided advertising support.

When I first started writing about the flex-shaft, I thought I knew quite a bit. However, while researching in-depth the abrasives, burs, motors, handpieces, etc., I was humbled in how little I knew. This book would still be an idea if it had not been for the guidance and patience in a barrage of constant questions. Thanks to the following people: Hanuman, Charles Lewton-Brain (who did a great job as the book's technical editor), Michael David Sturlin, Lorrie LeJeune, Jim Binnion, Doug Zaruba, Daniel Spirer, Elaine Corwin of Gesswein, Anne Hollerbach, David Olmsted, The Café on the Commons (where I spent countless hours writing and drinking coffee), and Sumner Silverman and Sally Pierce (who gave me their home on an island where much of this book was written).

I also wish to thank the Metalwerx Studiomates, staff, and faculty for borrowing their burs, abrasives, hands and workspaces for impromptu photography sessions. I also thank the members of the Orchid forum. Without you, this book would not have been written.

Foreword

In 1983, the prominent metalsmith and jeweler Harold O'Connor authored *The Flexible Shaft Machine: Jewelry Techniques*. Until now, it has been the only resource describing jewelry techniques for a flexible shaft and its components. However, innovations in the past couple of decades have led to huge leaps in the application and use of the flex-shaft, especially with finishing, drilling, and cutting of all types of materials. In this, the 21st century, the time has come for a new resource on the flex-shaft and its capabilities.

That resource—the book you now hold—arrived through the efforts of two of the industry's leading providers of technical and business information: Manufacturing Jewelers & Suppliers of America (MJSA) and The Ganoksin Project. In 2003, MJSA and Ganoksin formed an information-sharing partnership, and the alliance seemed only natural. As the trade association representing the U.S. jewelry manufacturing industry for over a century, MJSA has, among other initiatives, kept the industry informed about the latest developments in manufacturing practices and technology. It has achieved this through many means, most prominently through its award-winning flagship monthly magazine, *AJM: The Authority on Jewelry Manufacturing*; the books of MJSA/AJM Press; and, most recently, the educational programs of the MJSA Jewelry Academy.

Meanwhile, since its founding in 1996, The Ganoksin Project has created the industry's preeminent online resource. The brainchild of Dr. E. Aspler of Bangkok, Thailand, and Canadian jeweler and educator Charles Lewton-Brain, it maintains a substantial library of articles, publications, reports, and technical data, as well as numerous artist galleries. Among these resources are the archived e-mail postings of the "Orchid" forum, through which thousands of jewelers across the world have sought and found advice for a wide range of technical challenges. Over time, "Orchid" has come to represent the spirit of The Ganoksin Project's endeavor not just to supply information, but to foster a true community. The bonds of the "Orchidians" have even made the leap from the virtual world to the real world, and Orchid events now revolve like satellites around several of the industry's major trade shows and conferences (including the Tucson gem shows and MJSA's Expo New York).

The alliance has enabled MJSA and Ganoksin to disseminate technical information much more widely throughout the jewelry community. Until now, this has primarily been accomplished through each organization's respective Web site or the pages of *AJM* Magazine. *Making the Most of Your Flex-shaft* ushers in a new chapter in this partnership. It is the first in a series of books that will be published by MJSA/AJM Press under the "Orchid in Print" imprint. This series, titled "Maximum Bench Work," will enable the questions and discussions gleaned from the archives of the Orchid community to be preserved on the printed page. It will present insights into best bench practices that will help jewelers improve quality, speed production, and overall make their lives just a little bit easier.

While *Making the Most of Your Flex-shaft* began with a collaboration between MJSA and The Ganoksin Project, there were a few other collaborations without which this book would not have been possible. First, thanks must go to the book's prime sponsor, Rio Grande, as well as its patrons, The Foredom Electric Co. and 3M Inc. You can find more about these companies in the book's "Jewelers' Resources" section, which features some of the industry's leading suppliers.

Second, grateful recognition must go to the author, Karen Christians, who has done a masterful job presenting the intricacies of the flex-shaft in clear, concise prose (as well as taking the bulk of the photos). Her dedication to this project has been inspiring. She, too, has found this to be a highly collaborative effort (as she makes clear in her acknowledgments on page 6). And some of her greatest help and inspiration she received from the jewelers who participate in the Orchid forum. To them, we must extend our greatest debt of gratitude. Without their sharing and sense of community, this book and Orchid in Print would not exist.

Dr. E. Aspler (Hanuman)
Founder
The Ganoksin Project

Rich Youmans
Director of Communications/Publications
Manufacturing Jewelers & Suppliers of America

Web Apps

REMOTE ACCESS

SoonR

Get to your PC from any phone or browser

When you need remote access to your files but don't want to lug a laptop along, you need Soonr. This lightweight desktop utility syncs your files and Outlook email to SoonR's website while you're working and then serves them up via a clean web interface. The mobile-optimized service worked like a charm on every phone we tried it with, letting us grab and view images, Word docs, and spreadsheets easily. It also sports an organizer interface for Outlook calendars and lets you call your Skype contacts from your cell phone.

Free, www.soonr.com

VIDEO

Blinkx

12 million hours of video. No stupid self-submissions

Some people love whiling away the hours sifting through idiotic home-video footage on YouTube. If you don't, try Blinkx. Built on a powerful search engine, Blinkx scours the web for videos, then analyzes and tags them for retrieval. So when you search for "White Stripes," you'll find the band's videos, not a bunch of homemade vids of teenyboppers lip-synching to "Icky Thump." Blinkx grabs videos from across the entire web, so it's got everything YouTube, iFilm, Veoh, and the rest have, only more organized and with full-motion thumbnails. It includes a Safe Search control to filter out the dirty stuff—or not—and clicking a video's title will take you straight to its source, so you can see it in its original context.

Free, www.blinkx.com

Chapter One:
An Introduction to
the Flex-shaft System

The flex-shaft is a wonderful tool—but one that jewelers rarely use to its maximum advantage. Usually the first piece of serious equipment in which hobbyists or graduate jewelry students invest, the flex-shaft system makes bench work much easier: It reduces effort and fatigue, enhances production, and can be used for a variety of tasks, from scraping wafer-thin pieces of wax to grinding down larger pieces of metal for hollowware.

Despite this, the tool's accessories, power specifications, and range of uses have remained a mystery to many. This book is intended to solve that problem: It will attempt to demystify the flex-shaft system, and to educate each reader in how to use this essential tool to its full potential.

A Brief History of the Flexible Shaft

The first flexible shaft was invented by the famous Scottish engineer James Hall Nasmyth (1808-1890), best known for his later development of the steam hammer. In 1829, Nasmyth (Figure 1-A) worked as an assistant to the then well-known British machine tool maker and inventor Henry Maudslay (1771-1831). Years later, in a series of recollections, Nasmyth recounted his tool's development, reprinted here on page 10.

Figure 1-A

A Mode of transmitting Rotary Motion by means of a Flexible Shaft, formed of a Coiled Spiral Wire or Rod of Steel

"While assisting Mr. Maudslay in the execution of a special piece of machinery, in which it became necessary to have some holes drilled in rather inaccessible portions of the work in hand, and where the employment of the ordinary drill was impossible, it occurred to me that a flexible shaft, formed of a closely coiled spiral of steel wire, might enable us to transmit the requisite rotary motion to a drill attached to the end of this spiral shaft. Mr. Maudslay was much pleased with the notion, and I speedily put it in action by a close-coiled spiral wire of about two feet in length.

"This was found to transmit the requisite rotary motion to the drill at the end of the spiral with perfect and faithful efficiency. The difficulty was got over, to Mr. Maudslay's great satisfaction.

"So far as I am aware, such a mode of transmitting rotary motion was new and original. The device was useful, and proved of essential service in other important applications. By a suitably close-coiled spiral steel wire I have conveyed rotary motion quite round an obstacle, such as is indicated in the annexed figure [Figure 1-B].

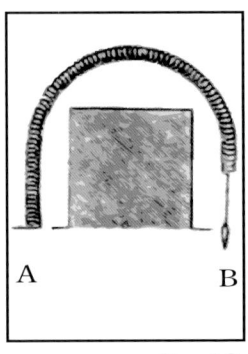

Figure 1-B

"It has acted with perfect faithfulness from the winch handle at A to the drill at B. Any ingenious mechanic will be able to appreciate the value of such a flexible shaft in many applications. Four years ago I saw the same arrangement in action at a dentist's operating room, when a drill was worked in the mouth of a patient to enable a decayed tooth to be stopped. It was said to be the last thing out in 'Yankee notions.' It was merely a replica of my flexible drill of 1829."

From this simple modification, the jeweler's flexible shaft was born. The modern flex-shaft can assist in many tasks, from drilling a hole to polishing metal to shaping wax. However, the myriad choices available in flex-shaft accessories—foot pedals, burs, abrasives, polishers, special attachments, specialty handpieces, and even the motor—can be daunting.

So what exactly is a flexible shaft? Actually, the term itself pertains only to one essential component of the whole system (the correct term is a "power rotary tool," but we will use "flexible shaft" or "flex-shaft" throughout the book). In total, the flex-shaft system consists of four components: the motor, the shaft itself, the handpiece, and the adjustable power source.

The Flex-shaft Motor

In its essence, the flex-shaft motor has one goal: to rotate the flexible shaft. It does this through the magic of magnetism—or, in this case, the manipulation of electromagnetism. Break apart the motor shell (Figure 1-C) and you will find two magnetic components. The first, called the "field," is fixed to the motor case. The second, the "armature," is a rotating electromagnetic cylinder wound with copper, which is centered on and fixed to the end of the motor shaft.

FIELD
BRUSH HOLDERS
COMMUTATOR
ARMATURE
MOTOR SHAFT
CARBON BRUSH
(FITS IN HOLDERS)

Figure 1-C

In the universal motor, the type most commonly found in flex-shafts, electrical current is introduced to the armature through the "commutator" (a cylinder comprising several insulated copper bars), which is mounted on the end of the armature. As current is applied, the armature is charged electromagnetically; the opposing polarities of the field and the armature interact—positive attracts negative, negative attracts positive—and the shaft begins to turn.

If the armature were allowed to turn without any further interference, eventually the polarities would align and the two magnets would repel each other. To offset that, the motor contains a set of carbon brushes that are mounted in holders on the inside of the case. As the armature rotates, the commutator's copper bars slide against the brushes, which *reverses* the direction of the current's electrons: positive becomes negative, and negative becomes positive. In this way, the polarities of the field and the armature are constantly alternating to ensure mutual attraction and continuous rotation, thus producing maximum motor torque.

Figure 1-D

The Flexible Shaft

The shaft, approximately 1 meter (3.3 feet) in length, consists of a solid steel wire core surrounded by two sets of coiled wires (Figure 1-D). The inner coil is symmetrically wound in a tight configuration from one end to the other, while the outer coil, or silencer, is loosely wound with approximately 1 millimeter (0.04 inch) between each coiled segment. This coiled shaft then fits into a flexible rubber sheath (Figure 1-E). (The degree of flexibility depends on the system's manufacturer.)

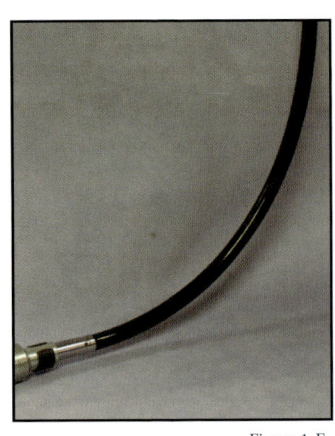

Figure 1-E

One end of the shaft has a thick-walled metal tube (motor coupling) that slips over the motor shaft and is secured by a setscrew (Figure 1-F). At the opposite end, the interior steel core wire extends past the coils about 2 centimeters (0.8 inch) and has attached to it a small piece of metal (Figure 1-G) that protrudes about 19 millimeters (0.76 inch) from the sheath tip (Figure 1-H). This metal tip acts as a "key" for the accurate mounting of various handpieces.

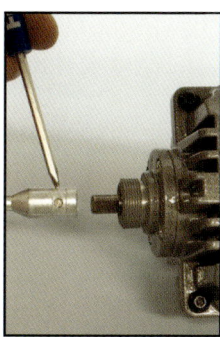

Figure 1-F

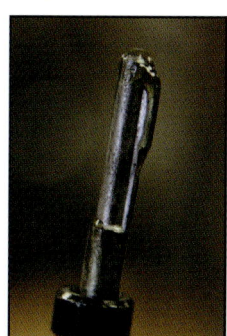

Figure 1-G

Figure 1-H

The Handpiece

The flex-shaft handpiece (such as the popular Jacobs Chuck, Figure 1-I, or quick-release handpiece, Figure 1-J) can hold various accessories, from burs and drill bits to brushes and polishing wheels. The flex-shaft handpiece is attached to the sheath by a spring clip and catch ball mechanism. Detailed descriptions of handpieces are found in Chapter 3.

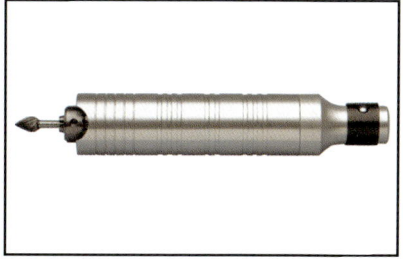

Figure 1-I

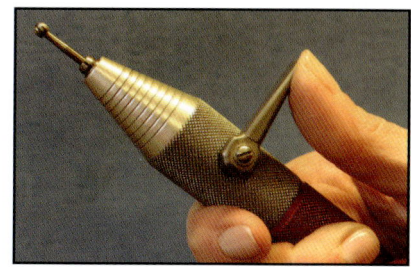

Figure 1-J

Figure 1-K　　　　　　　　　Figure 1-L　　　　　　　　　Figure 1-M

The Adjustable Power Source

To contol the flex-shaft's power, jewelers have several options: a foot pedal (Figure 1-K), a bench-mounted dial control box (Figure 1-L), or a dial control in the base of the flex-shaft (Figure 1-M). The speed at which the flexible shaft rotates is varied by the amount of pressure placed on the foot pedal, or by positioning the dial at a particular setting.

Systems in the Industry

As with so many other areas of the jewelry industry, many of the accessories, handpieces, and power systems were derived from the expanding technical innovations in the dental industry. Indeed, several brands of flexible shafts, such as Pfingst, Buffalo Dental, and Foredom, were initially created specifically for the dental market. Ultimately, goldsmiths discovered the advantages of the flex-shaft systems and began using them for polishing, detail work, and stone setting, among other repetitive applications. In the 1950s, artisan jewelers recognized the potential of the flexible shaft and began equipping their studios for polishing, texturing, and drilling. (Many novice jewelers have opted to adapt a Dremel hand tool, which is designed for craftspeople, as an inexpensive alternative to the flex-shaft. However, the Dremel's bulky motor in the constantly vibrating handpiece makes it uncomfortable for working on delicate jewelry over long periods of time.)

Today, a jeweler's bench is not complete without a flex-shaft system in place. Yet, before selecting a system, jewelers must ask many questions about their needs and which system will best meet them.

Chapter Two: Choosing the Proper Motor & Power Control

Determining the right flex-shaft for your work is much like choosing the correct vehicle for the kind of driving you do. If you haul large loads for your garden, or drive to craft shows, you will most likely choose a truck or a large van, rather than a sports car. In large part, your choice will be based on the vehicle's engine. Even though the truck and the sports car may have roughly the same horsepower, the two forces that make up that power—rotational speed (rpm) and torque—differ drastically. A truck motor with slower speeds will have higher torque, and the higher the torque, the more powerful it is for slower, heavy-duty work.

This same logic applies to choosing a motor for your flexible shaft system. If you use a flex-shaft only to drill the occasional hole or to sand the inside of a ring, then a smaller and lighter-duty motor will work fine. But if you're a full-time bench jeweler and use your flex-shaft every day to set stones or polish, then you'll require a higher torque and a more durable motor.

So how can you best match the right motor to your needs? First, you must understand the flex-shaft specifications.

Understanding the Flex-shaft Specifications

Whether in their catalog descriptions or on the labels attached to each flex-shaft, distributors and manufacturers will list important specifications about the systems they sell, including maximum speed (rpm), electrical power requirements (voltage and amperes, or volts and amps), and horsepower (hp). To make the most informed decision, every jeweler must know what those terms mean.

Horsepower. Defined as "work done over time," 1 horsepower equals 33,000 pounds per foot/minute. (Think of it this way: If you were to lift 33,000 pounds of books one foot over a period of a minute, you would have been working at the rate of 1 horsepower.)

Jewelry operations, of course, do not require 33,000 pounds per foot/minute, which is why most flex-shaft motors have a horsepower rating of $1/3$ or less. However, not all manufacturers rate their motor horsepower in the same way. A true continuous rating should represent the measured horsepower at the maximum efficiency point, i.e., the highest sustainable speed under a workload. However, some label markings represent the "maximum measured horsepower," which is simply the highest speed that the motor can go under no load. The motor cannot sustain this speed without overheating. If it's not clear how a flex-shaft motor's horsepower has been rated, always clarify with the distributor or manufacturer.

RPM (Revolutions Per Minute). RPM commonly denotes rotational speed—i.e., the number of times the shaft rotates in a minute. The motor label usually indicates the maximum rpm rating for the motor.

When comparing rpm among flex-shaft systems, remember that maximum speed does not equal maximum *torque*—the force applied by the shaft's rotation. This is where knowing horsepower comes in handy. You may see in a catalog a motor rated at $1/5$ hp and 5,000 rpm, and another rated at $1/5$ hp and 15,000 rpm. Although both motors are rated at the same horsepower, when they reach 5,000 rpm only one will have full torque; the motor that has a 15,000 rpm maximum will have just one-third torque, which may not be enough to do jobs with heavy workloads, such as grinding metal or heavy polishing. If a system cannot generate sufficient torque to overcome the workload, the motor will stall.

Volts and amps. A volt measures the force or push of electricity, an ampere measures the flow of electricity. Think of a water hose with one end attached to a fire hydrant and the other pointing toward a water wheel. The pressure behind the hydrant is your volt measurement; the amount of water released from the hose to turn the wheel is your ampere measurement. (Ohms, by the way, serve as your valve: They measure the amount of resistance used to regulate that pressure and determine the flow.) How many amps you will need depends on how difficult turning the water wheel may be—in other words, how much torque you'll need. For heavy-duty operations requiring more torque, you'll want a system with more amps.

AC current vs. DC current. AC, or alternating current, is found in your typical household outlet; it alternates the flow direction 50 to 60 times per second. DC, or direct current, has one flow direction.

A universal motor, the type most commonly found among flex-shafts, can use either AC or DC power. Permanent magnet (or PM) motors require DC power; they usually have a rectifier built into either the motor housing or the speed control to convert AC power to DC. The main benefit of a PM motor is it can produce more consistent torque at slower speeds, which gives the user more control in precision operations, such as stone setting, milling, drilling, and grinding. Low speeds can also help prevent points and bits from clogging when being used on soft metal, and they reduce heat buildup.

Finding the Right System for the Work You Do

Now that you have a better understanding of the motor specifications and what they mean, you can now determine the right motor for your needs. The table on page 18 shows the typical requirements based on the level of work involved.

Type of Job	Horsepower	RPM	Volts	Amps
Light Duty: Jobs that typically require higher speeds (e.g., polishing and drilling) with light to moderate tool application pressures (low torque needed) for short periods of time (one to three hours per day of continuous use).	1/10 hp universal motor	18,000 rpm maximum speed	115 volts	0.8 amps
Medium Duty: Jobs that typically require high to medium speeds (e.g., polishing, burring, drilling, applying high-speed abrasives) with moderate tool application pressures (medium torque needed) for long periods of time (one to five hours per day of continuous use).	1/8 to 1/5 hp universal motor	18,000 rpm maximum speed	115 volts	2.0 amps
Heavy Duty: Jobs that typically require high to low speeds (e.g., heavy polishing, grinding, burring, applying heavy-duty abrasives) with moderate to high tool application pressures for long periods of time (one to five hours per day of continuous use).	1/3 hp permanent magnet motor	15,000 rpm maximum speed	115 volts	2.6 amps

Bi-directional Motors

When selecting a motor, you will have a choice between unidirectional or bi-directional (i.e., reversible) motors. They offer some great advantages:

- *Ease in backing out drill bits from boreholes.* This is especially useful for lapidary work. If you've ever had a problem drilling a post-hole in an expensive stone, pearl, or intarsia pendant, then possessing a flex-shaft with reversing capabilities is priceless.
- *Greater control for left-handed operators.* While forward rotational direction provides the best tool control for right-handed operation, there are many lefties among bench jewelers. Also, forward direction cuttings can throw dust and debris into the operators face. With reverse rotational direction, that debris is thrown away from the user.

Reversible motors do have some drawbacks: fluted burs and drills will not cut in reverse, and changing direction too rapidly could damage the motor.

Foot Pedals

With your power requirements determined, you now need some way to control that power—in essence, you need a rheostat. As mentioned in Chapter 1, jewelers have three primary choices in this area: a bench-mounted dial control box, a flex-shaft-mounted dial control, and a foot pedal. While all offer advantages and disadvantages, most jewelers seem to opt for the foot pedal, which operates pretty much as the gas pedal on your car: Push down the pedal, and the shaft spins faster; let up on the pressure, and the shaft slows down. In addition to easy control, a foot pedal also keeps both of your hands continuously free, so you can hold or manipulate your work with one and grip the handpiece with the other, all while maintaining steady power control.

As do motors, foot pedals come in various forms. To choose the right one, you must consider the size and weight of your foot, the type of flooring under your bench, and the power of the flex-shaft motors. Some jewelers prefer cast-iron pedals (Figure 2-A). Because of their weight, these pedals require less pressure to hold them in the desired position, which greatly improves the tactile response to your foot and helps to maintain a steadier speed. This is particularly important for heavy-duty operations.

Figure 2-A

Figure 2-B

For other jewelers, pushing the heavier cast-iron pedals seems cumbersome; they prefer the "springier" feel of a plastic pedal (Figure 2-B), which is lighter but still very durable (and also less expensive). Plastic pedals could work well for someone with a small foot or who does mostly light-duty work. However, plastic pedals can slide away from you more easily, especially if they're resting on a linoleum surface. (Most plastic pedals are manufactured with an area for two screws, so they can be permanently mounted to the floor. Using Velcro tape also works well.)

Dial-Control Rheostats

Jewelers can also choose a rheostat with a dial control, which can be incorporated into either a benchtop control box (Figure 2-C) or the base of the flex-shaft motor (Figure 2-D). The dial operates in exactly the same way as the foot pedal, although it does offer advantages in certain operations. Possible oscillations in speed created by a foot pedal could hinder peak performance; a dial allows you to set one speed, at which the motor will run continuously. Also, when you use a hammer handpiece, a dial regulates a consistent speed while you move metal around a stone.

The disadvantage to a dial is that you have no easy way to vary the speed quickly. If you are exchanging abrasive accessories—say, from sandpaper to a setting bur, each of which needs a different speed—you need to dial in the correct speed each time, which is time consuming. If choosing a flex-shaft is like choosing a vehicle, then selecting a speed control depends on the type of trip you intend to take. If you are on a long cross-country journey, where you will be traveling on highways where the speeds will not vary for miles, you will want a vehicle with cruise control—essentially, a dial. But if you are winding through Big Sur, where speeds fluctuate constantly, then the foot pedal is the way to go.

Figure 2-C

Figure 2-D

Chapter Three: Choosing the Proper Handpiece

Open any jeweler's supply catalog to the section on flex-shaft handpieces, and you'll find a daunting array of choices. Some are long and slender, with springs on the end for flexibility; others are wide enough to accommodate large collets measuring up to a ¼ inch (6.35 millimeters) in diameter. Yet all of these choices can, surprisingly, be narrowed down to four main categories: Jacobs Chuck, quick release, collet, and hammering. Some jewelers even choose to keep several of these handpieces loaded at their bench at all times, so they can exchange them as needed. Understand these categories, and you'll be better able to select the handpiece that fits the job at hand.

The Jacobs Chuck Handpiece

The Jacobs Chuck handpiece is the most popular among jewelers for general use. Dating back to 1879, it is the invention of Arthur Irving Jacobs, the son of a Connecticut inventor and maker of round wooden pillboxes. According to the official Jacob Chuck Manufacturing Co. history, "The first Jacobs drill chuck was evolved, in a sense, the hard way. 'A.I.,' as he was nicknamed, was

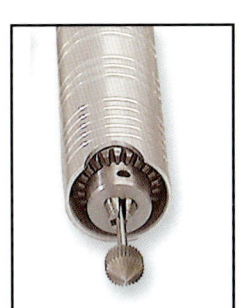

Figure 3-A

working with an old-type drill press, one hand holding the belt control and the other manipulating a spanner wrench to tighten the chuck, when, the wrench slipping, he barked his knuckles pretty badly. In a matter of days, however, Jacobs invented his first drill chuck with toothed sleeve and key complete. This was the foundation of the chuck business and solved a century-old problem, pioneering the drill chuck industry of today."

The Jacobs Chuck handpiece offers a nice combination of flexibility and ease of use. Because of the jaw assembly's system of integrated gears (see Figure 3-B), this handpiece can open wide enough to accommodate a range of standard mandrels, from ¹⁄₁₆ inch to ⁵⁄₃₂ inch

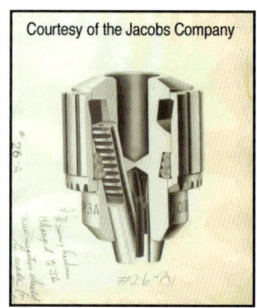

Figure 3-B

(1.6 millimeter to 4 millimeters), as well as various-size drill bits of up to ⁵⁄₃₂ inch. There are also several attachments that have been developed specifically for this handpiece, including drill presses, milling tables, wax lathes, and specialized stone-setting jigs, making the jeweler's work that much easier. (See Chapter 8, "Attachments for Your Flex-shaft," for more details.) And the Jacobs Chuck handpiece has permanently lubricated bearings, another advantage.

Figure 3-C

To open and close the tapered jaws around an accessory, jewelers use a Jacobs Chuck key (Figure 3-C). (For an image of the first Chuck key, see Figure 3-D.) The Chuck key has a set of gear teeth on one end, which correspond to a gear assembly in the handpiece itself. The "nose" of the chuck key rests in a small hole in the jaw (Figure 3-E), which provides a stable resting point as the gears are turned. There are three such "holes" around the exterior of the jaw assembly; to ensure the jaws close evenly around the accessory, you must tighten them equally. If you tighten only one, the accessory may spin out of balance or otherwise not run true, making precise work difficult.

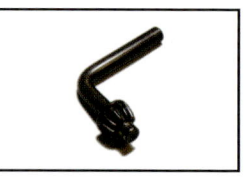

Figure 3-D

Overall, if your work involves a variety of tasks, necessitating mandrels and drill bits of different diameters, this is a good handpiece for you. Metalsmiths and jewelers often have several types of handpieces for their flex-shafts, and the Jacobs Chuck is usually among them.

Quick-Release Handpieces

Quick-release handpieces are also widely used by bench jewelers. Three types are available, each offering a different mechanism to tighten or release a mandrel or bur in the collet: a press-

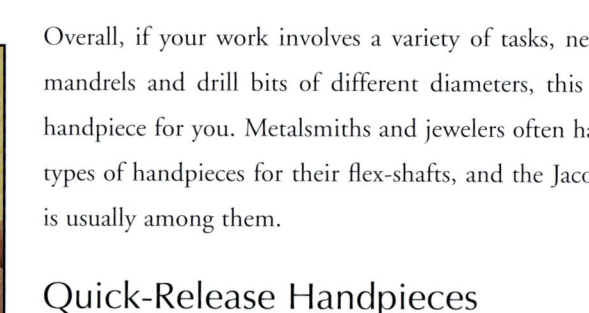

Figure 3-E

in/release lever (Figure 3-F), a lever that flips outward (Figure 3-G), and a push-pull sleeve (Figure 3-H). With them, jewelers can quickly change accessories and maintain a steady work pace. Also, unlike the Jacobs Chuck, which some find bulky in smaller hands, these handpieces come in smaller diameters (widths) and various lengths to accommodate different grips: You can hold them like a pencil, which gives you greater control for stone setting, delicate grinding, or abrading. However, the quick-release collet will accept only one mandrel size diameter, usually 2.35 millimeters or ³⁄₃₂ inch. You should also note that the spring assembly providing the quick release also places the handpiece collet under constant tension; to offset that tension, a mandrel or bur should be kept in the collet at all times.

Figure 3-F

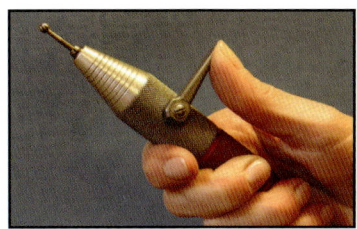

Figure 3-G

Figure 3-H

For greater flexibility, you can choose a quick-release handpiece with a duplex spring assembly (Figure 3-I)—basically, a handpiece with a spring inserted in the middle of its length, allowing you to angle the handpiece far more easily and offering improved access into recessed spaces. It offers several advantages:

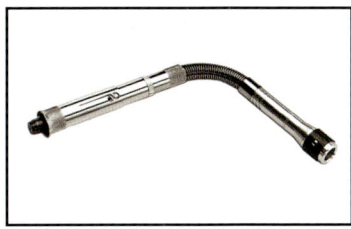

Figure 3-I

- Duplex springs provide you with extra flexibility between your handpiece and the shaft.
- Using a duplex spring assembly allows you to have tight curves and angles (up to 45 degrees) close to the handpiece grip, which is not possible with the flexible shaft alone.

However, duplex springs do require oiling to prevent them from heating up. Also, the springs can break from the constant bending and resulting stress, so more maintenance will be required.

Collet Handpieces

These handpieces use a variety of interchangeable collets that can match the diameter of the accessory being used. The ones for the smaller collet sizes (1/16 inch to 1/8 inch, or 1.6 millimeters to 3 millimeters) have slimmer grips suitable for more precise, delicate work. Other handpieces, which can hold larger shank accessories measuring up to 1/4 inch or 6 millimeters in diameter, are geared toward sturdier material applications, such as woodworking, glass cutting, and stone cutting. To change accessories, jewelers must use a wrench and pin to open and close the collet (Figure 3-J); however, that collet encloses the mandrel more thoroughly than the Jacobs Chuck. This collet style does not require a mandrel or bur to be inserted at all times.

Hammering Handpiece

This handpiece (known to many jewelers as a "hammer handpiece") is a specialized tool for stone setting and decorative applications. Designed to work at slow speeds (under 7,000 rpm), it acts literally like a small hammer head, and its anvil points (Figure 3-K) beat against the metal like a miniature jackhammer. A secondary adjustment on the handpiece changes the impact from hard to soft. Softer metals, such as high karat gold, will spread quickly, needing a slow but consistent speed. Harder metals, such as nickel white or lower karat gold, will need harder, quicker blows.

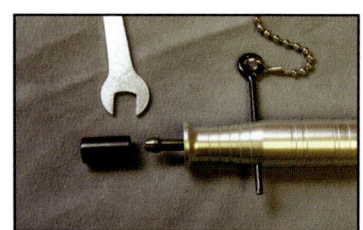

Figure 3-J

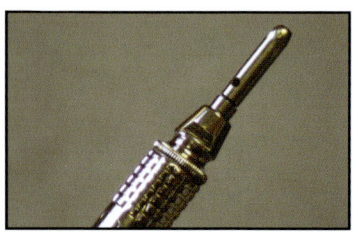

Figure 3-K

Using this handpiece takes the place of manually tapping a bezel closed or collapsing a rim of metal around a channel-set or flush-mounted stone. However, by using modified anvil points, jewelers can also use the hammering handpiece in prong settings. In addition, carbide- and diamond-tipped anvils are available for decorative work.

Choosing the Right Handpiece for Your Work

Once you know the four basic handpiece types, you can better determine which one is right for a particular job. Below are typical jeweler's tasks, with the corresponding handpiece that would best suit the work involved.

Cutting stone seats: Jacobs Chuck, collet (with rotary burs), quick release.

Drilling metal, stone, and pearls: Jacobs Chuck, collet, quick release (with rotary burs).

Decorating metals: Hammering.

Drilling with drill press: Jacobs Chuck.

Engraving/marking (rotary) on metal and glass: Jacobs Chuck, quick release, collet.

Engraving/stone setting: Hammering.

Grinding and removing heavy material: Jacobs Chuck, collet (heavy duty).

Hammer setting (bezel, channel): Hammering.

Jump Ringer System attachment: Jacobs Chuck.

Polishing and finishing metals: Jacobs Chuck, quick release (2.35 mm shank only).

Wax carving (with burs): Jacobs Chuck, quick release, collet.

Wax turning and shaping: Jacobs Chuck with Matt attachments (see Chapter 8, page 65).

Do's and Don'ts for Your Handpiece

Don't remove the black spring clip and steel catch ball at the end of the Jacobs Chuck handpiece; this mechanism secures the handpiece to the shaft and sheath.

Don't lubricate any of the handpieces. They all have permanently lubricated bearings. The only exceptions to this rule are the duplex spring handpieces and the hammering handpiece.

Keep a mandrel or bur loaded in a quick-release handpiece at all times.

Keep a backup of the handpiece you use most, in case it breaks down.

Wrap the handle in plastic wrap, if you are working with water for lapidary applications. Wipe clean and dry after each use.

Attaching the Handpiece to the Flex-shaft

Once you've chosen the correct handpiece for your needs, your next step is to attach it to the flexible shaft. This is a fairly simple procedure. First, look at the end of the shaft; you should see a small protruding piece of metal or "key" (Figure 3-L). This key lines up with a corresponding keyhole in the handpiece (Figure 3-M). To connect them, engage the motor until the key begins slowly rotating, then place the back end of the handpiece onto the shaft (Figure 3-N). The key is "self centering," which simply means it will automatically locate the keyhole in the handpiece.

When the chuck/collet begins to rotate, push the handpiece further onto the flex-shaft to lock them together. It might take a bit of force, so don't be concerned; when you hear the catch, you'll know the handpiece is secure.

To remove the handpiece, grasp the handpiece firmly in one hand. With your other hand, hold the end of the connecting shaft. Using some force, pull them apart.

Figure 3-L

Figure 3-M

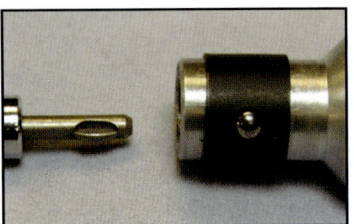

Figure 3-N

Chapter Four: Choosing the Proper Bur or Drill Bit

Of all the tasks requiring repetitive motion, removing metal is perhaps the one for which jewelers are most grateful to have the help of a flex-shaft. The amount of effort needed to scoop out or pare away a portion of even the most malleable alloys—particularly for such precise tasks as stone setting—makes the flexible shaft a true friend indeed. Jewelers just need to know the range of proper attachments—specifically, the drill bits and burs—available to them, and how to select the best one for the specific task at hand.

The Drill Bit

Ever since Stephen A. Morse opened the Morse Twist Drill and Machine Co. in New Bedford, Massachusetts, in 1864, the twist drill has become a staple of the jeweler's tool kit. With its concave corkscrew shape, this bit literally scoops out metal: The cutting edges (two opposing angled flat faces) bite into the metal's surface, and the rotation forces the shavings up the "flutes" (i.e., troughs) along the shaft. Among its applications:

- Stone setters will usually use a twist drill bit to begin a hole, to save wear on their burs.
- Twist drill bits can be used to create sized holes for rivets and wire, or to increase the diameter of existing holes. They can also be used as a type of rotary file for enlarging small openings (e.g., a rectangular slot) by moving the drill bit up and down slightly while at the same time pressing sideways.
- When they need to pierce a hole in the middle of a sheet of metal, jewelers will drill a pilot hole through which they can fit a saw blade.
- Although really considered more of an abrasive, the diamond-coated twist drill bit can be used to drill holes in stones and glass. Most diamond "drills" are really just a steel rod or tube with a few millimeters of diamond plated tip. They do not shave or cut material as a true drill bit does but grind it away.

Jewelers most often use the twist drill bit with a Jacobs-style handpiece, the jaws of which can tighten around the bit's shaft and hold it securely. Step-down bits, however, have a 3/32 inch (2.35 millimeter) shaft that's designed specifically for the quick-release handpiece, which has a collet of a corresponding size. Because of the difference in size between the 3/32 shank and the actual bit, care must be taken to ensure that the drilling is straight, or the cutting area of the bit will snap off.

Regardless of which handpiece you choose, the key is to select the correctly sized bit for the job at hand: whether creating an opening for a stone setting or for threading a wire, you don't want to remove any more metal than necessary. Twist drill bits are most often supplied to the jewelry industry in a progressive range of metric sizes, from 0.2 millimeter to 25 millimeters; they also may come in fractional sizes (from 1/64 inch to 1 3/4 inches in the U.S.) or American Wire Gauge (1 to 80).

When selecting a bit, always choose one that's slightly smaller than the hole you intend to create. If you require a large opening, say 15 mm, it would be inadvisable to begin with a drill bit of the same size, as it can easily catch the metal and twist out of your hands. Instead, begin by striking the hole's intended location with a center punch; the resulting dent will serve as a starting point for the tip of the bit. (Bypassing this step could cause the drill bit to skip and snap.) Next, choose a small bit to drill a pilot hole. You can now enlarge the hole with progressively sized bits, until you reach your desired diameter. As always, wear eye protection when performing any operation involving metal removal.

When drilling holes in pearls, jewelers will often turn to the spade bit. With their extremely sharp points (Figure 4-A), these bits enable stable contact with the pearl's round, slick contour, and their shapes are ideal for creating the necessary cylindrical opening. (The pointed end of the spade bit also eliminates the need to use a center punch, which could severely damage the pearl.) However, as with all burs, caution should be taken when using this bit: Because of its flanged

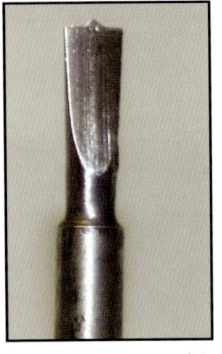

Figure 4-A

shape, the bur could overheat if used at high speeds. And if it does, the bit will lose temper—and once temper is lost, the steel becomes soft and the cutting edges lose their ability to cut cleanly.

Twist drill bits are almost always made of high-speed steel (HSS) or carbide, both of which can withstand high heat without losing temper. (This is especially important with tiny drill bits, which often require excessive speed that generate a great deal of frictional heat.) High-speed steel is less expensive and more forgiving, but carbide maintains its sharp edge for a longer time. Carbide also works better on harder materials. (For an overview of these two alloys and which works best with specific metals, see "Available Alloys" on page 36 and "Metal on Metal" on page 37.)

The Many Shapes of Burs

Like drill bits, burs basically cut and remove metal. However, they offer jewelers greater flexibility, since they come in a greater range of shapes, each designed for a specific task. For the relatively simple job of placing a diamond in a prong setting, jewelers will choose one bur to create the cavity (i.e., seat) for a stone, another to fine-tune the seat based on the stone's characteristics, and yet another to finish the prongs. They also must choose from among a range of steel alloys that offer longer wear and increased performance (see "Available Alloys," page 36, and "Metal on Metal," page 37). To make the best choice for the job at hand, you must understand the significance of each shape and alloy, as well as their best uses. (Just remember, when cutting a stone seat, always select a bur that is fractionally smaller than the stone.)

Note: Any heavy bur, from 4 millimeter diameter up, should have its shank shortened by about one-third to seat it more deeply into the handpiece; this will help to prevent it from bending suddenly and becoming a lethal L-shaped propeller.

Ball Burs

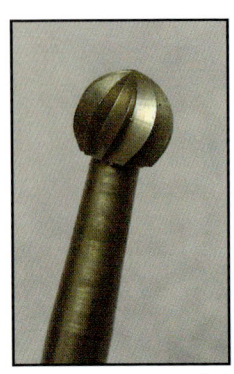

Figure 4-B

The simple shape of a ball bur (Figure 4-B) makes it extremely versatile, perhaps the most versatile of all the burs. Its uses include:

- Cutting to make curved surfaces.
- Faux carving, for surface texture or signatures.
- Expanding a hole.
- Providing an alternative to a drill bit for tight areas or fine gauge metal.
- De-burring the edges of a hole after drilling.
- Removing metal from and creating undercuts for the interiors of bezels and channels.
- Establishing a seat for a drill bit or another bur before drilling on a convex surface, such as half round stock and tubing.
- Refining a bearing seat where the stone will sit in the metal.

When using a ball bur, remember this one tip: Don't use the bur farther down than its equator or mid-line. Doing so will wear it out more quickly.

Setting Bur

Figure 4-C

The setting bur (Figure 4-C) is particularly useful for setting diamonds (although some jewelers I know prefer other bur shapes for this job). That's because its distinctive shape—a small cone that resembles an old circus tent, perched on a fat cylinder—allows the jeweler to cut a seat at the perfect angle for round, brilliant, symmetrical stones. It particularly shines when you need to cut a seat in a prong, a bezel, or a tube. (For channels, you'll want a hart bur.)

Hart (or Bearing) Bur

Unlike the setting bur, the hart bur offers jewelers three distinct angles from which to choose: 45 degrees (Figure 4-D), 70 degrees (Figure 4-E), and 90 degrees (Figure 4-F). For cutting channels, choose the 45 degree and 70 degree burs: Their acute contours bite a deep groove, allowing for stones to slide in easily. This is especially important when fitting on a curve, such as with a cast ring. When dealing with small, sturdy stones, such as diamonds, the hart bur's shape allows for the stones to be literally "snapped" into place. Other particularly useful applications include:

Figure 4-D

- Creating undercuts.
- Cutting seats in prongs and cutting notches (70 degree burs).
- Scoring and bending (90 degree burs).
- Creating seats for faceted stones with a sharp girdle.
- Creating textures.

Figure 4-E

Also note that hart burs are more closely calibrated than setting burs: Hart burs are made in increments of 0.1 mm; setting burs are sold in increments of 0.25 mm.

Bud Bur

Figure 4-F

The bud bur (Figure 4-G) gets its name from its "flower bud" outline. The cutting surface extends from its tip to the equator or centerline, and it creates a tapered hole with a slight curvature. Jewelers particularly love this bur for hinge openings. Other uses include:

- Shaping seats for stone shapes, such as marquise or cushion, with large, curved pavilions.

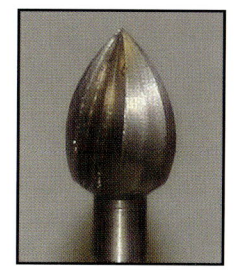

Figure 4-G

- Refining the interior surfaces of a flush-cut seat. In a pinch, you can also substitute a bud bur when you don't have access to a setting bur with the correct diameter.

In addition to their stone-setting applications, bud burs also come in handy for tasks in fabrication. It can be used to:

- Drill a hole in smaller gauge metals.
- Move a hole that has been incorrectly placed.
- Create a tapered hole that can be filled by a metal rivet (i.e., countersinking).
- De-bur and clean up holes.
- Create a concave flaring for tubing that will be used with hinges.
- Expand drilled holes

Figure 4-H

Flame Bur

With a longer and more slender shape than that of its cousin the bud bur, the flame bur (Figure 4-H) can prepare seats for small stones. It can also very lightly correct the placement of a hole, and is very useful in building catches and mechanical constructions.

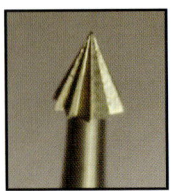

Figure 4-I

Cone Bur

The profile of a cone bur (Figure 4-I) is that of a solid triangular cone. Jewelers use these burs for tapering holes in a pin stem or a rivet, as well as for cleaning up the reverse side of a drilled hole. It's different from a bud bur in that, as it shapes an opening, it creates no curvature to the taper.

Figure 4-J

Inverted Cone Bur

This is an oddly shaped bur, but exceedingly useful. Shaped exactly like an upside down cone bur (Figure 4-J), the wider diameter is very good for undercuts, especially when you want the bottom of a seat to be flat.

Inverted cones are also great for:

- Cleaning up channel settings, or for channel inlays.
- Cutting tapered slots, similar to dovetail joints.
- Starting a seat in an irregularly shaped setting, such as a fancy-shaped bezel.
- Cleaning solder fillets inside bezels.
- Texturing surfaces.

Slim Reamer

A 45 degree triangularly shaped bur with a sharp cutting edge, the slim reamer (Figure 4-K) enlarges holes very efficiently.

Cup Bur

This bur has its cutting teeth inside its concave-domed shell, rather than on the outside as other burs do. It is used for:

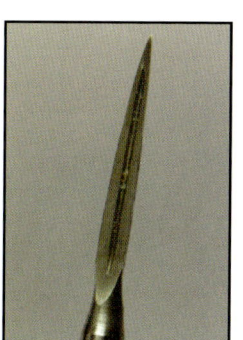

Figure 4-K

- Finishing prong tips into rounded ends.
- Rounding spheres.
- Rounding off the ends of ear wires.
- Shaping and polishing rivet heads. (For this task, use a dulled cup bur with ample lubrication, and apply steady pressure.)

There are two kinds of cup burs. One has multiple flutes (Figure 4-L), while the other—the "Champion" cup—has only two flutes (Figure 4-M), which alleviates the problem of the flutes clogging with metal.

Figure 4-L

In addition, because the Champion cup removes excess metal by shaving it away, instead of grinding or burring, it cuts faster and leaves a smoother surface.

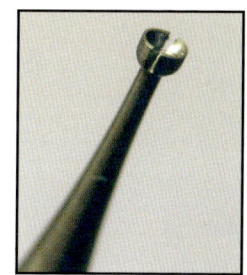

Figure 4-M

Wheel Bur

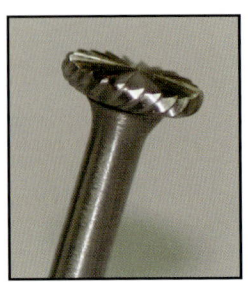

Figure 4-N

Used to remove metal from the inside of a bezel (particularly those with thick walls), a wheel bur comes in two versions. The round edge wheel (Figure 4-N) has flutes radiating from the center of the disc toward a gentle, rounded edge. The cylinder bur wheel (Figure 4-O) has flutes that radiate outward and down the sides at a sharp 90 degree angle. When do you use one over the other? The round edge wheel is good for cleaning up after holes drilled for bead setting. Its soft contour allows for precise removal of material without reshaping the opening.

Figure 4-O

Like the inverted cone, the cylinder bur wheel will cut a symmetrical seat in a stone for a cabochon. However, because it has teeth on both the tops and the sides, this bur has double cutting action. If you have a very thick walled bezel and need to remove a sizable amount of metal for the stone, this is a very good bur.

Krause Bur

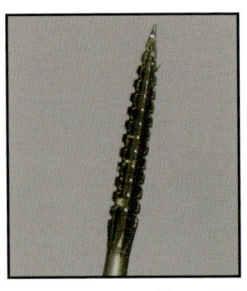

Figure 4-P

Certainly one of the more aggressive burs available for the flex-shaft, the sharp teeth of the Krause bur (Figure 4-P) chew away metal very precisely. The slim contour allows access to tiny recesses, and the gentle taper is perfect for installing hinges, for creating a notch for a prong setting, or for just slightly refining an end of the fitting. It's also great for cleaning up flashings in castings, where you need aggressive action in a tiny space.

The Krause is not commonly used in stone setting applications, but its shape does make it one of those useful burs required for repairs. One typical job a bench jeweler might have would be repairing box clasps in tennis bracelets. The protruding tongue in the box clasp usually poses no problem to reach, but when it comes to removing the stem soldered onto the bracelet link, the Krause's unusual shape comes in mighty handy.

Wax Burs

All of the burs listed above are certainly aggressive enough to cut through wax, but because their flutes are tightly spaced, soft wax will instantly clog them, rendering them useless for this task. Modeled after the contour of stone setting burs, wax burs (Figure 4-Q) have their flutes spread more widely apart, allowing for the wax to slide away. Most wax burs are made of tungsten vanadium.

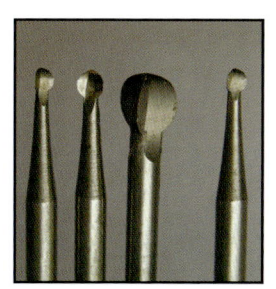

Figure 4-Q

Cylinder Bur

Also known as rotary files, these burs (Figure 4-R) are very helpful in grinding the inside of a ring shank and removing metal in instances where hand filing would take too long. Other uses include:

- Cleaning up sprues, solder spills, and porosity.
- Removing specific amounts of metal.
- Carving or smoothing waxes (if the bur is coarse enough).
- Carving into mokumé-gane to create patterns.

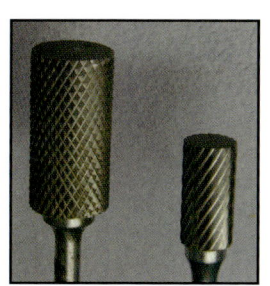

Figure 4-R

Cross-cut Cylinder Burs

These burs (Figure 4-S) are more aggressive than cylinder burs and are particularly good for cleaning, material removal, and casting cleanups.

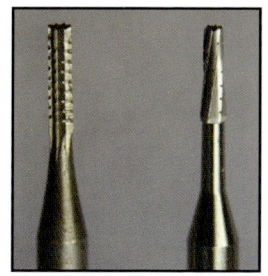

Figure 4-S

Figure 4-T

Florentine Burs

Solely used to embellish surfaces, the Florentine bur (Figure 4-T) comes in the shape of a flame, cylinder, bud, and barrel. It creates a lush satin finish of varying degrees of smoothness, similar to that left by a sand or bead blaster.

Keeping Burs Lubricated

Regardless of their differences, burs share one important characteristic: They all have flutes (troughs between the teeth) designed to move metal away from the work area. Because of this design, burs can fill with metal (or "load") while cutting. "Loading" occurs when metal residue packs the flutes (Figure 4-U), and excessive packing can lead to broken flutes and "smearing," or imprecise cuts. To offset this, jewelers should first lubricate their burs. Lubrication allows the metal residue to slide from the flutes, carrying away heat energy and extending the life of the bur. Jewelers have many options among lubricants, from light oils (including mineral, sewing machine and tap and die oils) to commercial waxes, such as Bur Life and Bur Cut. If your bur chatters or screams, it needs lubrication.

Figure 4-U

Available Alloys

In addition to a broad range of shapes, burs also come in a variety of alloys. When choosing from among these alloys, jewelers should determine how best to balance the cost, wear, and performance characteristics of each. For example, a specialized industrial alloy such as tungsten vanadium steel was designed specifically to help jewelers make more precise cuts—but it wears out quickly, and its cost, while initially cheap, will add up over time.

To help you make those choices, the following page offers some of the more common steel alloys found among burs (as well as drill bits).

Carbide steel: A combination of cobalt and tungsten, this alloy gives bits and burs longer-lasting tips, sharper cutting edges, and greater impact resistance. The advantage of using carbide steel is that it maintains a sharp edge, even when hot. The disadvantage is its cutting action. Although sharp, carbide chews away at the metal, rather than delicately abrading. Carbide burs also cost more than burs made from other alloys. For maximum performance, you should run carbide burs at very high speeds of 30,000 rpms or more.

Vanadium steel: With steel, there is always a trade-off between hardness and toughness; as a steel alloy hardens, it also becomes more brittle. Tungsten vanadium steel was created to make burs both harder and tougher. This alloy allows manufacturers to grind more flutes on the burs, allowing jewelers to make more precise cuts. This is particularly useful for stone setters, as is the alloy's ability to grind seats and remove metal at very slow speeds—far below the requirements for carbide steel. Yet while vanadium steel burs are cheap to purchase (about half the price of tungsten carbide or high-speed steel), they do wear out quickly, which is why you often buy them six in a pack.

High-speed Steel (HSS): High-speed steel is formulated to withstand frictional heat up to 1,000 degrees Fahrenheit without softening.

Titanium-nitride-coated HSS: A metal formulation that is harder than tungsten carbide and very resistant to abrasions. It's ideal for metal cutting and drilling, since it generates less heat.

Metal on Metal

So which bur and bit alloys work best on which metals? Most jewelers agree that high-speed steel is the best all-around alloy for gold, silver, platinum, white gold, copper, and brass. High-speed steel is more forgiving, has less chatter, and, because you pay more for them, they are usually better made. However, even HSS burs can dull faster in lower karat gold, such as 14K. (Remember, you must lubricate any bur.)

Metal	Bur/Bit Alloy	Cautions
Gold	Carbide, High-Speed Steel, Vanadium	Wax lubricant acceptable. Do not run at high speeds.
Nickel Silver	Vanadium, Titanium Nitride	Work slowly. Use oil lubricant, rather than a wax lubricant; waxes will heat up and evaporate too quickly.
Silver	Carbide, High-Speed Steel, Vanadium	Wax lubricant acceptable. Work at medium speeds.
Platinum	Carbide, Vanadium	Platinum tends to grab the drill bit or the bur, so work slowly. Lubricate liberally.
Copper	Carbide, High-Speed Steel, Vanadium	Wax lubricant acceptable.
Brass	Carbide, High-Speed Steel	Wax lubricant acceptable. Work at medium speeds.
Bronzes	Carbide, Vanadium, Titanium Nitride	Lubricate liberally. Work slowly.
Aluminum	High-Speed Steel	Lubricate liberally. Work at low speeds. Aluminum is soft and can clog flutes. If same bur or bit is used with other metals, it can contaminate them.
Titanium	Carbide (preferably), Titanium Nitride	Heat travels slowly on titanium, and the bur alloy could lose temper if run at high speeds. Lubricate liberally and run at low to medium speeds.
Pewter	High-Speed Steel	Tin can clog flutes easily, so lubricate liberally. To avoid contamination, don't use the same bur or bit on other metals.

For deep and significant cutting on materials such as mokumé-gane or steel, you would use carbide. (Carbide is also great for rotary files.) The nature of the carbide allows you to apply pressure when using it, since it is very sharp and durable. Cut slowly, though, because carbide is also very brittle: Use it too fast and you can shatter the teeth and lose the temper in the steel. You'll want to run your flex-shaft at medium to high speeds, with plenty of lubrication, and bring the bur or bit slowly to your metal.

Vanadium burs have smaller teeth, so they don't chip as easily. Because they cut slowly and can be run at lower speeds, they are easier for most setters to control. If you compare them with other burs, you will find that they are more closely calibrated to the proper size.

The chart on page 38 further defines which bur alloys you should use when working on specific metals.

Chapter Five: Choosing a Mandrel

Regardless of its size, shape, or application, every flex-shaft accessory has one common characteristic: It needs an attached shank that can be inserted into the handpiece. That means that before jewelers can begin working with buffs, polishing wheels, and abrasives, they must select one more accessory: the mandrel.

Mandrels are small metal rods of various widths, constructed of either stainless steel or nickel-plated base metal. (Stainless steel costs more, but it is also more durable.) The rod or shank is completely smooth for insertion into the handpiece, while the top end has a screw head or slot for mounting the buff, polishing wheel, or abrasive. Mandrels come in various configurations, but in the end the choice involves personal preference. This chapter focuses on a few options.

Standard Mandrel or Screw Mandrel

This simple mandrel is designed for either the Jacobs Chuck or the collet-style handpieces. They are available in several standard shank diameters: $3/32$ inch, $1/8$ inch, $1/4$ inch, $1/16$ inch, 2.35 millimeter, 3 millimeter, and 6 millimeter, with wide or narrow heads. Mandrels with a wide screw and shoulder head (such as those in Figure 5-A) provide added support to larger accessories, which helps them to run true with less flexing.

Figure 5-A

When choosing your mandrel, you will also need to match the arbor screw diameter with the size of the accessory mounting hole. If the arbor screw is too small, the accessory will wobble and not run true. Mandrel arbor screws are available in $1/16$ inch, $1/8$ inch, and $1/4$ inch diameters with standard right-hand threads. There are even specialized left-hand-threaded screw mandrels available for running the flexible shaft in the reverse rotational direction.

When using this mandrel, you must pay particular attention to the load you place on the head. If you are using a hard acrylic wheel, a compact fiber wheel, or a Mizzy wheel and are creating additional load, a reinforced stainless-steel mandrel with a large head would work best for your task. But if you are performing a light application and using a small radial bristle disc or a light muslin buff, you can choose the less-expensive nickel-plated mandrel with a smaller head. (Using a smaller head is perfect for the tiny radial bristle discs, which are designed for smaller crevices; a large screw head might inadvertently grind into the work.)

Most standard mandrels sold are mounted on removable accessories, which have tiny screw threads attached. However, some come with permanently mounted accessories, such as silicone polishers, steel/brass brushes, or cutting discs (Figure 5-B); once the accessories wear out, they, along with the mandrel, are thrown away. Although they cost more, these mountings allow for more torque to be placed on the accessory.

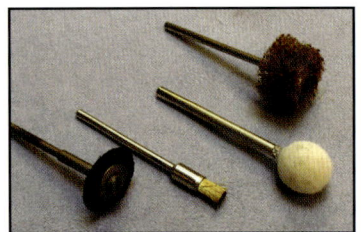

Figure 5-B

Snap-on Mandrel

Specifically designed for snap-on abrasive discs, this mandrel (Figure 5-C) has a specialized head that snaps onto the disc. It cannot be used for any other accessory. (See Chapter 6, "Abrasives and Grinding Wheels," page 51, for more about snap-on discs.)

Figure 5-C

Disc Mandrel

A variation on the snap-on mandrel, this mandrel (Figure 5-D) has a flexible backing to accept diamond and silicon carbide finishing film abrasives. Designed for tasks that require a more delicate hand, this fixed mandrel style allows the user to bear down with increased torque.

Figure 5-D

Split Mandrel

Available in two shapes, tapered (Figure 5-E, left) and cylindrical (Figure 5-E, right), this slender shank is "split" above its reinforced base, creating a gap through which jewelers can wind paper-like or cloth-based abrasives, such as sandpaper, belt sander strips, and polishing papers. (There is also a quarter-inch split-mandrel that's been developed specifically for micro-finishing film.) The cylindrical mandrel is perfect for finishing inside rings or other smooth surfaces, while the tapered version, with its tapered, pointed end, offers access to undercuts and other small areas.

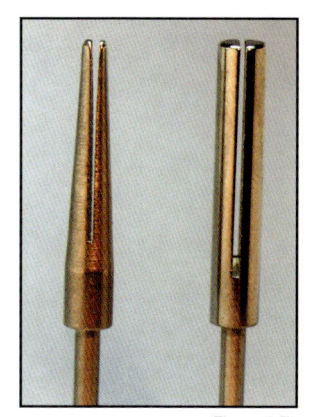

Figure 5-E

Note: Any heavy mandrel, such as a split mandrel, should have its shank shortened by about one-third to seat it more deeply into the handpiece; this will help to prevent it from bending suddenly and becoming a lethal L-shaped propeller.

Drum Arbor

With its stout, round shape and thick mandrel rod, the drum arbor can take more torque than other mandrels, making it particularly suitable for heavy-duty cleanups. It can reach deeply recessed spaces more effectively; if you need to finish inside a ring or the lip of a small vessel, you'll want the drum arbor. It has a fixed rubber drum that allows the abrasive (specifically designed for this tool) to slip on and off with ease. When using this accessory, the abrasive band should first be slipped onto the rubber drum, then the arbor screw should be tightened. This causes the rubber drum to expand in diameter until the abrasive band is held firmly in place on the mandrel. Drum arbors come in a great variety of sizes and shank diameters. For an exploded view showing the individual components of this accessory, see Figure 5-F.

Figure 5-F

Spiral or Tapered Mandrel

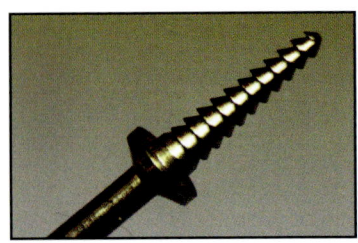

Figure 5-G

The tapered mandrel (Figure 5-G) holds polishing accessories with vertical shapes (e.g., felt or rubberized cones or cylinder). Because it has an open thread with no head, the jeweler can simply screw the polishing accessory directly onto the mandrel. The spinning accessory then tightens itself on the widening threaded taper. This open-thread design also provides great stability throughout the length of the cylinder. Tapered mandrels come in a variety of tapers (wide or thin) and shank diameters. There is even a left-handed threaded version for when you want to reverse the rotational direction. Sometimes a drop of glue in the hole will keep such a mounted accessory from stripping its threads while in use.

Polishing Point Mandrels

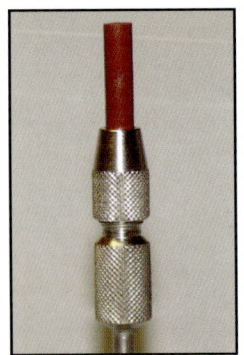

Figure 5-H

Available for 2 millimeter and 3 millimeter diameter rods, these mandrels have jaws into which jewelers can screw either ceramic mini-point abrasives or cylindrically shaped acrylic or rubber polishing rods (Figure 5-H) for working on very hard and dense metals, such as nickel white gold, platinum, and titanium.

Chapter Six: Abrasives & Grinding Wheels

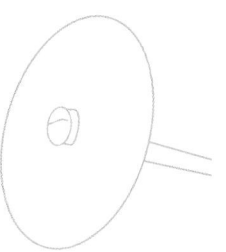

Where would the jeweler be without the wide variety of abrasives available today? From innovations such as 3M's Scotch-Brite Radial Bristle Discs to diamond-impregnated wheels, points, and burs, these abrasives allow jewelers to grind, scrape, smooth, and polish all kinds of metal. They can even, in the case of diamonds, drill and polish gemstones and glass. In short, these and the other abrasives can be viewed as the workhorses in the jeweler's arsenal of flex-shaft accessories.

The most common abrasives used in the jewelry industry are aluminum oxide and silicon carbide. Aluminum oxide—a sharp, hard abrasive made by subjecting the mineral bauxite to high temperatures—works particularly well in pre-polishing operations, since it leaves deep scratches in the metal's surface. (Corundum, which includes ruby and sapphire, is the crystalline form of aluminum oxide; with a hardness of 9 on the Mohs scale, the mineral makes for a potent abrasive, and it serves as a component in many cutting tools.)

Silicon carbide works even better for cutting hard materials than aluminum oxide, as it is 9.5 on the Mohs scale—it will even carve into ruby and sapphire. A fusion of silica and coke (a byproduct of coal), this black, iridescent abrasive splinters during use and creates finer scratches than aluminum oxide.

Other abrasives offer their own advantages; each deserves a prominent place in your toolbox. However, to get the maximum benefit from them, you first must understand their individual characteristics, as well as the various forms in which they're available.

Abrasives at a Glance

Abrasive	Ceramic (aluminum fiber and synthetic polymer; porcelain and diamond)
Available as...	Knife-edge wheels, points, cylinders, square-edge wheels; common trade names include Foredom CW wheels, 3M Purple Ceramic bands and discs
Works well on...	Hard, dense metals—e.g., platinum, titanium, steel
Good for...	Pre-polishing, removing scratches, dressing tool steel for punches; maintains crisp contours on steel stamping tools

Abrasive	Wax/tallow with various abrasives (including silicon carbide, aluminum oxide, chrome oxide)
Available as...	Polishing compounds
Works well on...	Each compound is metal specific
Good for...	Pre-polishing, final polishing

Abrasive	Diamond
Available as...	Drill bits, adhesive-backed pads, "burs," hollow cores, cut-off wheels, rubberized points, film, bands, discs
Works well on...	All metals, all gemstones (including diamond), glass
Good for...	Drilling through glass and stone, pre-polishing, final polishing, cutting

Abrasives at a Glance

Abrasive	Silicon carbide
Available as...	Heatless wheels ("Mizzies"), separating discs, snap-on discs, sandpaper, polishing papers, 3M EXL wheels, 3M Micro-finishing Films
Works well on...	All metals, as well as all gemstones except diamond
Good for...	Pre-polishing and polishing

Abrasive	Aluminum oxide
Available as...	Separating discs, cut-off wheels, sandpaper, snap-on discs, 3M Micro-finishing Film discs, sheets and bands, and 3M Radial Bristle Discs
Works well on...	All metals
Good for...	Pre-polishing, removing scratches, texturing

Abrasive	Rubber with abrasives (e.g., aluminum oxide, silicon carbide, pumice, diamond)
Available as...	Points, cylinders, knife-edge wheels, square-edge wheels; common trade names include Cratex, MetalMaster, Brightboy, AdvantEdge, and Edenta
Works well on...	Silver, gold, brass, copper
Good for...	Removing scratches, light deburring, creating soft contours (coarser grits); applying pre-polish and final polish (finer grits)

Figure 6-A

Figure 6-B

Figure 6-C

Figure 6-D

Sandpaper

For jewelry/metalsmithing applications, the most versatile abrasive is sandpaper (Figure 6-A), also known as "wet-and-dry" for its ability to be used when wet, thus reducing the number of abrasive particulates thrown into the air. Available in various grits (usually from 80 to 600), it can be loaded into a split mandrel and used to even out scratches on the metal's surface. Jewelers normally proceed from rougher to finer grits; the lower the grit level, the rougher the abrasive. A typical progress would be 220 to 320 to 400 to 600 grit.

Before using this sandpaper, you must first break the glue backing to make the papers more pliable. To do this, take the strip you plan to use and, holding each end, drag the paper downward, abrasive side up, over a sharp 90 degree surface edge. You can do this on either your bench pin (Figure 6-B) or, better yet, a steel bench block. This will break the glue and allow the paper to spiral, making it easier to load onto the mandrel.

Now, with the abrasive facing upward, load one end of the sandpaper into the mandrel (Figure 6-C), until a quarter inch sticks out of one end. Keeping your thumb against the paper, slowly increase the speed of your flex-shaft until the paper wraps around the mandrel (Figure 6-D). Apply water to the piece on which you're working, and you're ready to begin abrading. (If you use belt sander material known as "shop roll," the glue on this material is designed to run hot and the abrasive grit stays on for far longer than it does on sandpaper.)

3M Wetordry Polishing Papers

These flexible papers (Figure 6-E) have taken the buffing process, formerly a tedious chore done with large machines, and brought it to the bench with the aid of a flex-shaft. As with sandpaper, these papers can be mounted in a split mandrel, but the abrasive load can reach much higher than that of wet-and-dry sandpaper.

Made of very fine grade silicon carbide and a high-grade aluminum oxide, these flexible papers measure about 8 ½ inches x 11 inches, the size of a standard piece of copy paper. They are coated in varying concentrations of abrasives that are measured in microns (see sidebar, "Microns vs. Grit"; unlike with grit measurements, the lower the micron measurement, the finer the finish). If translated into sandpaper grit, these concentrations would range from 400 to 8,000 grit—far exceeding the 600 grit limit found in most sandpaper.

Always use a moderate to high speed when abrading with these papers. Because they are very soft—they have the flexibility of a paper towel—they will give a very good final polish on all metals.

Figure 6-E

Microns vs. Grit

In standard sandpapers, the grades run from lower to higher numbers (e.g., 120, 220, 320, 400, etc.). This number corresponds to the amount of abrasive distributed on the surface. For example, a 120 grit sandpaper has an estimated 120 particles of aluminum oxide per square inch. Consequently, to cover the paper equally, those particles need to be larger than the particles found in 220 or 320 grit papers. The higher the grit number, the smaller the grit size.

3M Wetordry Polishing Papers, on the other hand, are graded in microns. This measurement reflects the size of the abrasive particles, not the quantity. The lower the micron abrasive, the finer the abrasive.

Below is the range of available papers.

Green	30μ
Gray	15μ
Blue	9μ
Pink	3μ
Mint	2μ
Pale green	1μ

3M Scotch-Brite Radial Bristle Discs

Figure 6-F

Developed from larger discs manufactured for the auto industry, these discs (Figure 6-F) were introduced by 3M to the jewelry industry in 1995 and have since swept the industry by storm. Theses flexible plastic discs are impregnated with aluminum oxide grain of various grits; the abrasive concentrations are identified by color-coding. These discs are especially useful in that they can reach into tiny crevices around prong settings, undercuts, and other areas often inaccessible by other means. Other applications include:

- Removing firescale
- Removing solder fillets
- Evening out scratched surfaces
- Creating texture
- Smoothing surfaces

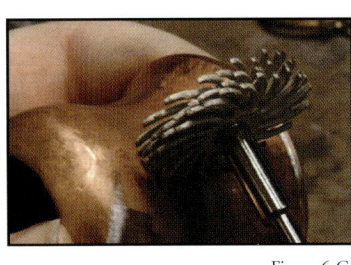

Figure 6-G

To achieve the proper results, you must use a stack of at least three to six discs (Figure 6-G). Do not run one disc alone, since this would offer little stability and induce the tendency to push too hard on the disc. (As when using a file or a saw blade, jewelers should let the abrasive do the work.) You must also stack the discs in the same way, with the 3M logo facing downward.

As with polishing papers, the Radial Bristle Discs should be operated at moderate to high speeds (lower speeds will give poor performance). Also, be aware that the bristles will break off with use; when the discs wear down to the hub, replace them. The bristles may discolor and become darker over time, but don't worry; that will not change the effectiveness of the product. (If they're wearing away fast, you're probably pressing too hard.)

Snap-on Discs

Also called "Moore's discs" or "sanding discs," these small round discs (Figure 6-H) can abrade difficult-to-reach areas quite well, since their flexible backing (either plastic or paper) allows them to bend to oddly shaped surfaces. The disc is usually placed with the abrasive surface facing inward, toward the handpiece, for greater control. The available abrasives are usually either silicon carbide or aluminum oxide (such as Adalox).

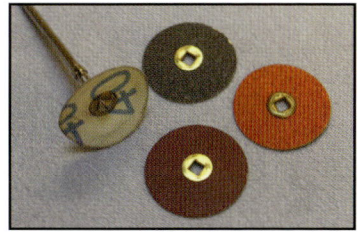

Figure 6-H

However, these discs can't be used with just any mandrel; they contain a square brass insert that matches a mandrel specifically designed for it. For more information, see Chapter 5, "Choosing a Mandrel," page 42. (Note: In addition to snap-on discs, there are also old-fashioned-style discs available, with a simple hole that fits the standard screw-mount mandrel.)

3M Micro-finishing Film

The aluminum oxide abrasive on this film (Figure 6-I) has a very precise size and distribution. This gives the film an advantage over more common abrasives, such as sandpaper, which are layered electrostatically with aluminum oxide and resin—a process that distributes

Figure 6-I

the abrasives at different angles or in a random manner. The film's greater consistency reduces the amount of pressure needed to achieve a smooth and consistent finish.

The 3M Micro-finishing Film is best used flat and wet. It also comes in a disc form that attaches to a special adhesive-back mandrel (see Chapter 5, page 42). These discs allow you to better bear down when you require extra torque, such as when finishing curved surfaces. (Note: this film is now also offered in small bands in various micron grades.)

Figure 6-J

The film fits quarter-inch split mandrels (Figure 6-J) specifically designed for this product.

Polishing Compounds

Polishing compounds consist of an animal-fat binder combined with various waxes and/or abrasives, such as aluminum oxide, iron oxide, or chrome oxide. There are about 25 kinds of polishing compounds; depending on the size and variety of the abrasives used and the formulas in the binders, the applications range from removing scratches on steel hammer heads to applying a lustrous final finish on platinum.

Also available are "water soluble" compounds (a bit of a misnomer, since fats aren't really soluble in water), which have the exact same formulation as the regular compounds except for one thing: They have an added ingredient that allows rapid breakdown in water, enabling faster, easier cleanup.

These compounds are usually applied by brushes and buffs. For more detailed information about compounds, see Chapter 7, "Buffs, Brushes, & Polishing Compounds," page 60.

Diamond Abrasives

In lapidary applications, steel won't cut through stone. But diamond, as the strongest material, will — just as it will abrade just about every other material. Excellent at grinding, drilling, polishing, and texturing, these abrasives come in a variety of forms suitable for

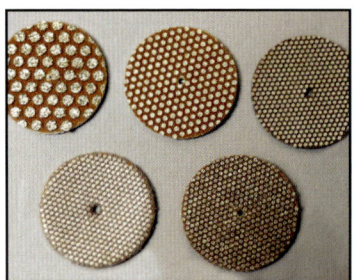

Figure 6-K

the flexible shaft, including adhesive-backed discs (Figure 6-K), as well as drill bits, hollow cores, and burs (Figure 6-L). 3M Flexible Diamond abrasives also come in sheets and bands, as well as discs.

Diamond abrasives comprise multiple layers of diamond particles over a steel shank that has been either shaped on a lathe or milled with a CNC machine. The particles are usually applied in one of two ways: by nickel plating, in which the plating holds the abrasive onto the steel, or by sintering. In this second process, the shank is fired in a mold, with the diamond bits adhering to the lathed form through heat and pressure. Sintered bits cut slower than those that are plated, but are more durable and have a longer life.

Figure 6-L

A few guidelines when working with diamond abrasives:

- Proceed slowly when using a diamond abrasive to drill through glass or stone. Run the flex-shaft at no more than 1,000 rpm and lower the rotating abrasive gradually onto the surface, or you will run the risk of cracking the piece.
- Make sure that, when working with a diamond abrasive, you apply water to it either by submerging the tool or by running a continuous drip. This will prevent it from overheating and allow it to last longer.
- Drill incrementally, lowering and raising the bit to release the slurry that builds up.

Heatless Wheels

Thick-edged heatless wheels (Figure 6-M) are good for texturing surfaces or preparing edges for soldering. Known as "Mizzy" wheels, these silicon carbide accessories can also efficiently grind down the edge of a sprue, and are particularly useful in the metalsmithing application "marriage of metal," in which the parent metal is pierced and metal of another color is soldered in its place. Where a Radial Bristle Disc gently abrades, the Mizzy's gritty surface aggressively chews metal and makes great textures. However, unlike burs, they do not load or catch, nor do they need lubrication. They work best at slow to medium speeds on your flex-shaft.

Figure 6-M

Separating Discs and Cut-off Wheels

A concentrated form of the same aluminum oxide or silicon carbide compositions found in sandpaper, separating discs (Figure 6-N, left) and cut-off wheels (Figure 6-N, right) are delicate and friable, but very useful nonetheless: They cut material where a saw blade cannot. They are especially great for cutting a stack of jump rings on a wooden dowel, or for scoring and bending applications.

Figure 6-N

Separating discs and cut-off wheels have minimal differences. Cut-off wheels are generally a bit more expensive, and some wheels are made of diamond-coated metal. The real choice lies in the abrasive. Silicon carbide discs and wheels, while less expensive, are also extremely thin and break easily. For the extra money, aluminum oxide wheels and discs last longer. They also come in larger diameters, and have a longer mandrel that puts the handpiece farther from the work at hand (thus minimizing the chance of an inadvertent slip of the handpiece that would mar the metal's surface).

Compressed Fiber Wheels

Compressed fiber wheels, such as the 3M Unitized Wheel (Figure 6-O), are constructed of compressed, non-woven, tough abrasive fibers bonded together with an adhesive system under heat. The wheels are then cut from a solid block. The end result: an extremely long life. They work particularly well for removing firescale, deburring, applying a pre-polish, and removing the parting lines on a casting. For flex-shafts, they are available as wheels (for standard mandrels) or as fixed mounted points in various shapes. For operations in which high torque is needed, the fixed point mandrels work best.

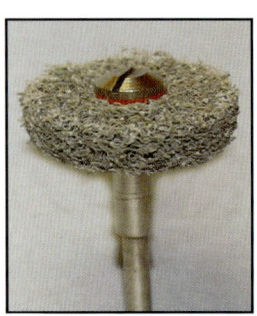

Figure 6-O

Rubberized Points and Wheels

Rubberized points and wheels offer substantial access to deeply recessed crevices, such as those between prongs, and can be altered in shape for specific problems (you can grind them on the teeth of an old file). They can also nicely cover large surface areas, such as a hefty bezel or the back of a belt buckle.

The key is in selecting the proper abrasive material. Aluminum oxide points and wheels work well for significant metal removal: They can readily take away separation lines from castings, as well as small flashes of excess metal or solder spills. Many of these accessories are known by their brand names. Cratex wheels (Figure 6-P), for example, are among the more well known; they abrade metal exceptionally well, allowing the refinement of a curve or a contour.

Figure 6-P

Those accessories impregnated with silicon carbide or diamond, on the other hand, usually have a finer grit and can take over for the polishing stage. Widely recognized brand names include Edenta and AdvantEdge, both of which offer a high-quality rubber and an especially even distribution of the abrasive particles. When choosing the abrasive, be aware that the harder the material, the more friction it can withstand. (Diamond, of course, would rank at the top.)

Another good abrasive for rubberized wheels is pumice. A popular polishing compound, pumice is often sold as a powder that can be mixed with water and applied manually for pre-polishing. However, the combination of pumice (in the form of a rubberized wheel) and the high rotational speed of the flex-shaft allows you to achieve a lustrous high polish for gold or silver. (Pumice wheels are also safe around most stones.) Since it wears down quickly, you don't want to use a pumice wheel in production runs. However, it is a perfect accessory for those who create the occasional piece of gold or silver jewelry.

Ceramics

The term "ceramics" is actually a catch-all that refers to two different kinds of materials: one porcelain-based with diamond, the other a combination of alumina fiber and synthetic polymer (epoxy resin). Both are suitable for the final polishing of prongs and fine details.

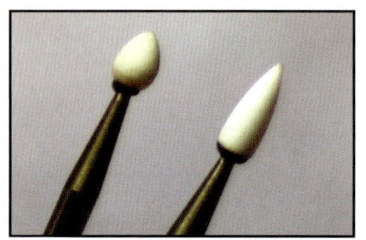

Figure 6-Q

Originally intended for the dentistry market and adapted by jewelers, porcelain polishing tips (Figure 6-Q) are work well in tiny areas with undercuts. They can be used on precious metals for achieving a final finish, since the porcelain's smooth exterior does not significantly move metal. (They are also excellent for polishing small details in stone or shell.)

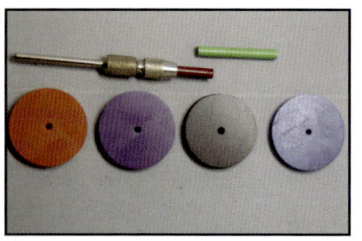

Figure 6-R

The alumina fiber/synthetic polymer combination (Figure 6-R) comes in the forms of rods and wheels. Styled for the final finish of larger surface areas, they work best on the upper speeds of your flex-shaft (again, metal movement is minimal).

Both materials are extremely hard and don't break down under heat and pressure.

3M Trizact Abrasive

Figure 6-S

Well-suited for pre-polishing or for sanding curved objects, this abrasive contains multiple layers of pyramid-like structures (Figure 6-S), allowing fresh mineral to be exposed after each use. The structure also wears evenly, produces less loading, and produces a faster cut. Trizact is available in belts, bands, discs, and rolls.

Chapter Seven: Brushes, Buffs, & Polishing Compounds

When discussing polishing and buffing, you're really talking about reflection, the play of light on a surface. A polished effect depends on two things: the structured organization of the surface's molecules, and the smoothness of the surface. Think of a molecular lattice structure as a military operation, with each atom a foot soldier. When everyone is in perfect alignment, the effect is symmetrical and balanced. Combine such an organized structure with a very smooth surface, and you get a mirror polish. A satin finish would result if the surface has more texture.

The flex-shaft enables you to achieve this. Chapter 6 presented the various abrasives that jewelers use to help them with polishing and texturing metal, among other tasks. In this chapter, we'll focus specifically on buffs and brushes designed for the flexible shaft, as well as the polishing compounds used with them; when joined with the abrasives, they form a potent arsenal that will help any jeweler achieve the desired final finish.

Natural Bristle Brushes

Traditionally, brushes laden with polishing compound offered a way to finish a piece of jewelry, and they are still used by many jewelers. Available in different shapes—cylinder, cone, or wheel—they allow for access into tight corners and undercuts.

Brushes take basically two forms, natural bristle and wire. Bristle brushes (Figure 7-A) come in three levels of flexibility: stiff (made of hair from a horse's tail),

Figure 7-A

medium (made of hair from a horse's mane), and soft (made of goat hair). Another natural brush material is tampico, which comes from the agave plant in Mexico. It is a soft to medium fiber with good durability.

Usually used with bobbing compound, bristle brushes allow the jeweler to pre-polish a piece. They are very good for patterned metal, as they don't affect the delicate surface. To use them properly, you should let the tips do the work and not apply too much pressure. Optimum operating speeds will vary, depending on the type of compound and the metal you are working on. However, higher speeds (10,000 to 18,000 rpm) seem to give better results.

Wire Brushes

Figure 7-B

Wire brushes, which impart a surface texture rather than deliver a high polish, come in two levels of flexibility: stiff (0.005 inch bristles) or soft (0.003 inch bristles). Brass wires (Figure 7-B) give a light satin finish, whereas steel wires (Figure 7-C) give a much deeper and defined texture. With brass wire brushes, many jewelers use soapy water as a lubricant to avoid leaving residue on the metal.

Figure 7-C

Remember, you should never run the brushes faster than their maximum recommended operating speed. Also, you should wear a face shield, as the tiny wires can come loose and hit you in the face.

Texturing Wheels

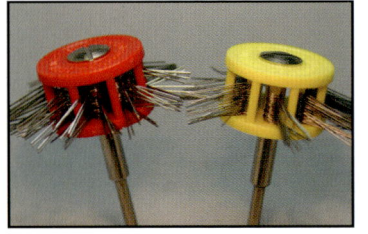

Figure 7-D

Texturing wheels (Figure 7-D) have small, stiff metal wires attached to a plastic core. They impart a pebbled finish very similar to that achieved with a sand or bead blaster.

Note: Flex-shaft manufacturers have concerns over this tool, since the currently available versions have 3/32 inch or 2.35 millimeter shafts, which are too weak for higher rpm; the high speeds could bend the shank into an L shape and turn it into a dangerous propeller. Suitable texturing wheels should have 1/8 inch or 3 millimeter shafts and be run at very slow speeds (around 2,000 rpm). Also, a face shield must be worn if you use this tool.

Stitched and Unstitched Buffs

Stitched buffs (Figure 7-E) in either muslin or finished cotton are the means to the final polished finish. Stiffer cotton buffs, like muslin, create greater friction and heat, causing the polishing compound to heat up and allowing the abrasive to do its work. This combination of speed, heat, and compound creates a kind of slurry, causing the crystalline structure of metal to line up in formation. Stitched buffs work well with Tripoli or White Diamond compounds for cutting and pre-polishing. The stitch count varies with different buffs; the higher the count, the greater the friction (e.g., a six-stitch buff will create more friction than one with three stitches).

Figure 7-E

Floppy and soft, unstitched buffs (Figure 7-F) work best with final polishing compounds, such as rouge or platinum white. These compounds are usually softer; their organic binders are meant to break down more quickly, allowing the fine polishing particulates to work against the surface.

Figure 7-F

Felt Buffs

Figure 7-G

Because of its unique compressed structure, the felt buff (Figure 7-G) creates the highest heat and friction of any buff. Cutting compounds used with this buff can cause drag lines and even facets on the metal's surface, so caution is recommended. Felt buffs work well for the fine, controlled finishing of a variety of metals—including harder or denser metals, such as platinum, steel, and titanium.

Chamois Buffs

Figure 7-H

Originally made from goat skin, this buff (Figure 7-H) works well when you want a high luster finish. It is very flexible, to the point of being floppy, and often comes with a stiffer material inside to help support the outer material.

Polishing Compounds

There are really only two types of polishing compounds, those that cut and those that polish or "color." However, the common use of Tripoli or bobbing compound (for cutting) followed by rouge (for high luster) is not always the right choice. Careful reading of polishing compounds will help you decide which is the right one for you.

Jewelers can choose from a wide range of compounds, including many proprietary brands; you must carefully read the information provided by each supplier. The table on pages 61 and 62 can help you with this decision.

Compounds at a Glance

Type	Cutting
Compound	Tripoli
Apply with	Muslin or cotton buff, brushes
Uses	Gives a smooth, satin finish on all metals, and removes light scratches, imperfections, and oxidation on non-ferrous materials. Medium cutting action.
Type	Cutting
Compound	Bobbing
Apply with	Muslin or cotton buff, brushes
Uses	Recommended for silver, brass, and copper to remove scratches and firescale. Leaves a dull finish. Greater cutting action than that achieved with Tripoli.
Type	Cutting
Compound	White Diamond
Apply with	Muslin or cotton buff, brushes
Uses	Will cut and gloss in one operation; provides a moderately high shine. XXX White Diamond is used to cut gold, silver, brass, copper, and plastics. XXXX White Diamond has finer abrasives that don't cut as well but provide better color.
Type	Cutting
Compound	Gray Star
Apply with	Muslin or cotton buff, brushes
Uses	Can be used to cut and color metal in one step, rather than two operations.
Type	Buffing
Compound	Red Rouge
Apply with	Buffs (usually cotton), felt wheels
Uses	Traditionally made of iron oxide. Darker-colored, coarser grains are used for grinding; finer grains are used for polishing steel and precious metals.

Compounds at a Glance

Type	Buffing
Compound	Green Rouge
Apply with	Buffs (usually cotton), felt wheels
Uses	A chrome oxide primarily used to apply a final finish on stainless steel, steel, brass, aluminum, nickel, and chrome. Also imparts a high luster to rhodium, platinum, chrome, and other hard metals.

Type	Buffing
Compound	White Rouge or Platinum White
Apply with	Buffs (usually muslin), felt wheels
Uses	Produces a bright high polish. Primarily used in the final finish of steel, stainless steel, and zinc. Also used on platinum. This compound is a favorite in coloring aluminum and brass.

Type	Buffing
Compound	Orange (Carrot) Rouge
Apply with	Buffs, felt wheels
Uses	Designed specifically for platinum; it produces a bright white finish with a subtle luster.

Type	Buffing
Compound	Black Rouge
Apply with	Buffs, felt wheels
Uses	Produces a deep finish on silver and pewter.

Type	Buffing
Compound	Blue Rouge or Platinum Blue
Apply with	Buffs, felt wheels
Uses	Produces a very high luster.

For more information, see "Notes about Buffing and Polishing Materials" by John Fisher, which has been posted on the Ganoksin site at *www.ganoksin.com/borisat/nenam/buffing-material.htm.*

Chapter Eight: Attachments for Your Flex-shaft

The flex-shaft and its accessories will definitely enhance your ability to complete repetitive tasks. Yet you don't have to stop there; you can extend your capabilities even further with the help of a few attachments designed specifically for the flexible shaft. They are available from most tool suppliers.

Drill Press

An adaptation of an electric drill press, this accessory (Figure 8-A) extends the flexibility of the Jacobs Chuck handpiece. It features a lever to raise and lower the handpiece, a table for mounting the work, and a depth gauge for repetitive drilling tasks. Either a foot pedal or a dial control will work very well with your flex-shaft and Jacobs Chuck handpiece in the drill press. Wax carvers also use this tool for milling and truing their filing waxes.

Jump Ring Cutting Jig

If you want to fabricate custom jump rings, whether in multiples or just a few, this attachment offers a speedy way to do it. It features a customized cutting jig and a small high-speed steel saw that can zip through many jump rings at a time. The most widely known brand name is the Jump Ringer (Figure 8-B).

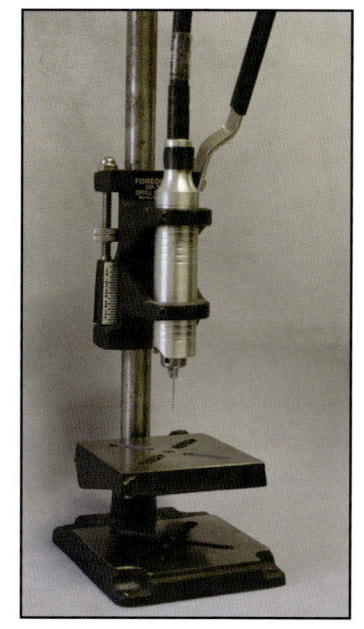

Figure 8-A

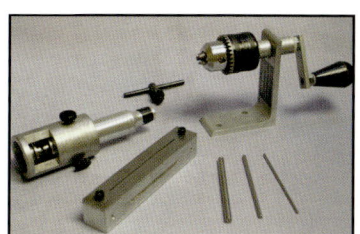

Figure 8-B

Figure 8-C

The AllSet Setting Guide System

Foredom's AllSet System (Figure 8-C) offers several setting guide sets and attachments, each specifically adapted for the Jacobs Chuck handpiece, which give the user greater flexibility and accuracy in cutting seats for prong, pavé, cluster, and channel settings. In addition to increasing the number of stone seats that can be cut quickly, thus reducing your labor costs, the AllSet System also offers additional advantages. By allowing the guides to position the setting burs, you can reduce the wobble that usually stems from your holding the handpiece. They will also help reduce strain placed on the hands.

You can also purchase setting guide kits for the Foredom No. 52, No. 18, and No. 10 (or Faro quick-change) handpieces that include a channel setting kit and interchangeable heads, as well as a prong-setting guide table that connects directly to these handpieces.

Figure 8-D

Milling Table

This is another application of an industrial tool that's been miniaturized for the flex-shaft, adapted for a small studio, and standardized for the jeweler or model maker. A milling table (Figure 8-D) enables you to achieve perfectly flat surfaces with heavier metal stock, such as tubing, shaped rod, or flat sheet. For those jewelers who have trouble maintaining a steady grip on the handpiece, it offers a great alternative. In addition, it allows you to create 45 degree bevels for locket and box constructions, a task that can be difficult to do by hand for even the most experienced artisan.

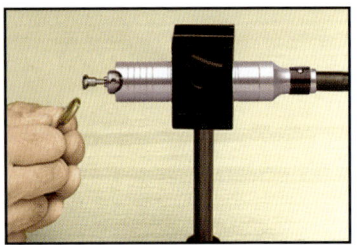

Figure 8-E

Handpiece Holder

Adapted for the Jacobs Chuck handpiece, this holder (Figure 8-E) fits securely into a vise for hands-free work.

Matt Wax Lathe

This hand-held lathe (Figure 8-F), powered by your flex-shaft, is designed to turn rods of carving wax and produce bands, bezels, and settings with accuracy and speed. It features a precision gauge for measuring exact dimensions, including the thickness of the work, eliminating the need to measure for proper widths. Specialty blades allow you to shape a ring band into many designs. Attachments include the Matt Wax Trimmer (Figure 8-G) and the Matt Bracelet Shaper (Figure 8-H), giving you the added flexibility of precision cutting and filing.

Wolf Belt Sander

Using 1 inch by 10 inch (2.5 centimeter by 25.4 centimeter) belts, this sander (Figure 8-I) fits onto a flex-shaft with a quick-release collar. It can be clamped onto a table or a bench, and can be adjusted to a variety of angles. Developed by Wolf Tools, it comes with five assorted belts. An optional mounting attachment is also available for use with the GRS Benchmate.

Figure 8-F

Figure 8-G

Figure 8-H

Figure 8-I

Chapter Nine: Maintenance & Safety Procedures

The flex-shaft will provide years of performance, as long as it's maintained properly. But it should not only be maintained carefully, but be handled with care as well. Never forget that we're talking about a piece of equipment that spins burs, drill bits, abrasive discs, and other sharp objects at thousands of rpm; it takes only one careless move to inflict major injury to you or a co-worker.

Fortunately, by following a few simple guidelines, you can ensure that both you and your flex-shaft enjoy a long, *healthy* life.

Maintenance Procedures

Note: Before beginning any maintenance operations, always make sure your power tool is unplugged!

You should routinely clean your flex-shaft system. This is especially true if it's operated in work areas that generate a lot of dust: Dirt and improper lubrication are the most common causes of poor operation and excessive wear. Typically, slots in the motor housing provide the airflow needed to remove waste heat and cool the windings. If sawdust and conductive debris (such as metal filings and gold dust) enter through these slots, they can collect and form a bridge between parts, causing an electrical short. In high dust environments, air should be blown through the motor (Figure 9-A) after every 40 hours of use. Canned air, the type used by

Figure 9-A

Figure 9-B

Figure 9-C

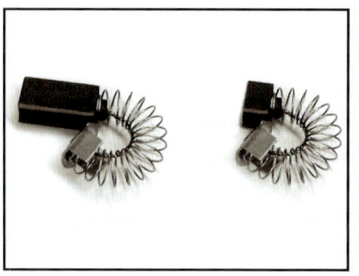

Figure 9-D

Figure 9-E

photographers and computer technicians working on printed circuit boards, works very well for this.

You should also periodically check the motor brushes for wear. To do this, unplug your motor and unscrew the motor brush caps (located on the motor's side, Figure 9-B). Carefully pull out the motor brush assembly (Figure 9-C). When new, each brush measures approximately ¾ inch or 19 millimeters long (Figure 9-D, left) and should be replaced when it wears down to ¼ inch or 6 millimeters (Figure 9-D, right). When replacing the brushes, match up the curvature on the motor brush end to the curvature of the armature (Figure 9-E). (For additional information about the armature and motor brushes, see Chapter 1.)

You should also regularly care for the shaft itself. It should be checked, wiped clean, and lubricated with grease after every 50 hours of use. Use flex-shaft grease or high-quality white lubricating grease. Note that only the shaft should be lubricated, not the motor. The same holds true for most handpieces; only the duplex spring and hammering handpieces should be lubricated, according to the manufacturer's instructions.

When lubricating the shaft, follow these procedures:

1. Remove the handpiece.
2. Loosen the set screw on the motor connector (Figure 9-F).
3. Slide the sheath out of the motor connector (Figure 9-G).
4. Apply a very light coating of lubrication to the shaft (Figure 9-H). With your gloved fingertip or a small brush, spread the lubricant along the shaft (Figure 9-I), starting at the top and working downward to about 1 inch from the end. Don't worry about spreading the grease now because once the machine is running, the motion will spread and redistribute the grease along the shaft. Be careful, though; if you apply too much grease, the excess will work its way into the handpiece and eventually seep out between it and the sheath. For this reason, apply a bit less as you approach the bottom of the shaft, near the handpiece. Also, never operate the motor with the outer sheath removed; this can be very dangerous.
5. Replace and adjust the sheath so that the shaft key tip extends between ¾ inch and 1 inch beyond the sheath (Figure 9-J). It should not extend beyond 1 inch.
6. Re-tighten the set screw in the motor connector.
7. Wipe clean the exterior of the sheath with a cloth.
8. Manufacturers suggest hanging and running the motor for about 10 minutes before re-attaching the handpiece. This will allow enough time for the

Figure 9-F

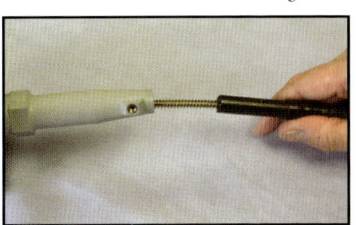

Figure 9-G

Figure 9-H

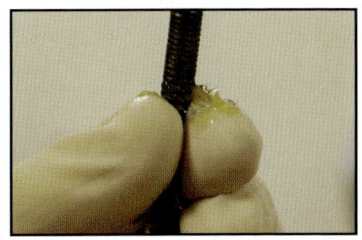

Figure 9-I

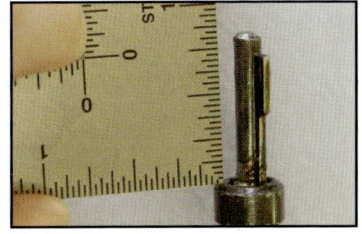

Figure 9-J

grease to warm up, spread, and drain off. Wipe off any excess grease at the tip end of sheath.

9. Re-attach the handpiece.

With every 200 hours of use, the shaft should be thoroughly cleaned with solvent, such as paint thinner, before being lubricated. In a well-ventilated area, pour 1 inch of paint thinner or other solvent into a plastic bucket. Disconnect the shaft completely from the motor, then place it, coiled, in the bucket. Take a worn, soft toothbrush and lightly brush the coils. After cleaning, place the shaft on a layer of either old newspaper or paper towels. Allow it to air dry for a minimum of 10 minutes. You are now ready to lubricate the shaft and put it back on your flex-shaft. (When using flammable solvents, take suitable safety precautions.)

Maximizing the Flex-shaft's Operation

While routine maintenance is crucial, you almost must operate the system correctly to ensure its continued health. When using the flex-shaft, keep in the mind the following important guidelines:

- When in use, the shaft itself should be slack, appearing as a gentle arc. If you bend the shaft too sharply and strain it, it will grind against the sheath and wear it down. This will greatly affect performance.

- When you engage a system with a foot pedal, the motor may twist slightly from the rotating commutator. This is completely normal. Make sure nothing will impede this motion, and that clear space surrounds the unit at all times. (This will also help to ensure the motor can give off heat and receive proper airflow.) Using a fixed hook to hang the flex-shaft is preferable to using a chain, which amplifies the twisting.

Safely Operating the Flex-shaft

In addition to following the guidelines above for proper maintenance and operation, also incorporate the following safety cautions, courtesy of noted goldsmith/teacher/author (and safety guru) Charles Lewton-Brain:

- Always wear eye protection. Face shields are recommended over safety glasses for chip-forming work. A jeweler that Charles knew once wrote to him, "I have a scar on my cornea from a metal splinter that got past my safety glasses. Since I have gone exclusively to a face shield I have had no serious eye injury." Some jewelers wear both safety glasses and a face shield for added protection.

- Use hearing protection, particularly with high-pitched sounds, such as burs on metal.

- Always take the key out of the Jacobs chuck after you use it—there have been some bad accidents when a tool was turned on with the chuck key in place.

  Never start the Nos. 10 and 20 "quick change" handpieces with the chuck or collet lever in the "open" position.

- Never wear dangling jewelry or any type of loose clothing that might become caught in the equipment. Keep your hair tied back.

- Do not place a tool that is too long or too heavy in the handpiece; it could suddenly bend to a right angle and become a fearsome propeller. A student of Charles's once put a round needle file into the flex-shaft for use as a bur; once the motor engaged, the file suddenly bent to a 90 degree angle and almost sliced off his nose as it knifed through the air.

- Brace the hand holding the workpiece against a bench pin. Better yet, clamp the piece securely in a vise or engravers block.

- Check working heights and positions. To avoid strain, make sure you don't bend your wrist much when using the tool.

- Never use a drill or accessory that appears to be wobbling out of round, vibrating, or not running true.

- Wear a dust mask appropriately rated for the particulates that will be produced from the task at hand.

- Finally, a personal note from Charles: "I still remember vividly the day I learned to use eye protection (and tie my hair back) when using a flex-shaft. I was 18 at the time, had long hair, and goldsmiths considered eye protection almost wimpy. Then, while using a bur one day, a tendril of my hair snapped around the tool. I can still clearly see the saw teeth of the bur winding rapidly toward my eyeball. I stopped it some millimeters from the eye, and I've worn safety glasses ever since. The embarrassment of having a flex-shaft handpiece attached to one's head can be acute—not to mention dangerous."

Chapter Ten: Beyond the Basics

So far, this book has presented the basics of choosing, using, and maintaining your flex-shaft system. But jewelers are a creative bunch, and for every standard practice they will usually find at least 10 new ways to modify, circumvent, or totally re-create the established practices, all in the pursuit of better doing their jobs. This chapter offers a few of those ideas, all culled from MJSA's flagship monthly magazine, *AJM: The Authority on Jewelry Manufacturing*, and The Ganoksin Project Web site, *www.ganoksin.com*. You'll never find them among standard flex-shaft instructions—but they could make your life a lot easier.

A 60-Second Tube Setting

Tube settings are an elegant way to add height and intrigue to a finished jewelry piece. They can spice up toggles or add decorative architecture to a ring. But the best thing about tube settings is that they're quick and easy to make. With a few simple tools and your handy flex-shaft, you can fabricate tube settings in a jiffy—60 seconds to be exact.

Andy Cooperman of Seattle—professor of metals, goldsmith, studio jeweler, and contributor to the Orchid e-mail forum on www.ganoksin.com—demonstrated the tube setting technique described here at a pre-conference workshop for the 2002 SNAG (Society of North American Goldsmiths) Conference in Denver. This time-saving technique takes advantage of the versatility and speed of the flex-shaft. It's suitable for use on diamonds, sapphires, rubies, or any lab-grown stones that can withstand the heat from torch soldering.

My studio-mate, Jamie Sachs, tested this technique. He had never previously fabricated a tube setting, but created one perfectly using this method. It's truly a bench tip that's eye-opening for novices and professionals alike.

To perform a tube setting using this technique, you'll need the following tools:

- A setting bur and a ball bur appropriate for the size of stone you are setting.
- A #30 Foredom handpiece.
- Lubricant.
- A gemstone (cabochon or faceted).
- A vise or Benchmate.
- Gold, copper, sterling silver, or brass tubing.
- A brass or steel burnisher.

Figure 10-A

1. Select the appropriate size setting bur for your stone. In this example, I am using a 3.5 millimeter machine-faceted natural blue sapphire and sterling silver tubing that has a 4.07 millimeter outside diameter and a 3.27 millimeter inside diameter. Cut the tubing to 6 millimeters and insert it into the #30 handpiece. Leave about 3 millimeters to 4 millimeters exposed.

2. Insert the ball bur into a Benchmate or vise and fasten securely (Figure 10-A).

Figure 10-B

3. This may seem contrary to the way you normally do tube settings with your flex-shaft, but it works well: Rather than attempting to balance the setting bur in one hand and the flex-shaft in the other, grip the flex-shaft handpiece in both hands. This balances your center of gravity over the setting bur.

4. Ream out the tubing with the ball bur (Figure 10-B). Doing so establishes a center point in the tubing for

the setting bur. It also chews away excess metal, thus extending the life of your setting burs. Once you've reamed out the tubing, replace the ball bur in the Benchmate with the setting bur. With the rotating tubing still in the handpiece, lower the tubing onto the setting bur and cut the seat for the stone.

5. To quickly determine the correct depth of the setting, just rest the stone on the tubing with the culet pointed upward; because the tubing is secure, there is no need to use wax to position the stone. The girdle of the stone should sit just below the rim of the tubing. At this point, the walls of the tube are ready to collapse around the stone. Flip the gemstone back over when ready to set it.

6. The next step is the beauty of this technique. The tubing and the stone are already in the #30 handpiece. Slowly increase the speed on the flex-shaft by pressing ¼ of the way down on your foot pedal.

7. Hold either a burnisher or a flat brass sheet against the wall of the tubing (as demonstrated in Figure 10-C) Slowly push against the wall of the tubing while it is rotating. *Voilà*—the stone is set (Figure 10-D).

Figure 10-C

8. Polish to the desired finish. Make sure the abrasive you are using is softer than the gem you're setting. Personally, I often use 3M polishing papers for this step. I tape them to a piece of wood to create a handy tool for polishing metal.

Now look at your watch. You'll be amazed how little time has gone by since you started this project. I suggest practicing a few settings in brass at first, but you'll be a pro in no time!

Figure 10-D

Flexing the Boundaries

A few tips from author/educator/goldsmith Charles Lewton-Brain, who is renowned for his "out of the box" thinking:

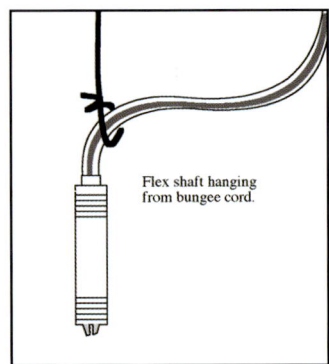

Figure 10-E

- When using your flex-shaft to set stones, try this trick for greater steadiness. Tie a bungee cord to the ceiling directly over the bench pin. When you need to use a vertical drilling motion, tie the bungee cord to the flex-shaft hose just above the handpiece (Figure 10-E); the resistance as you pull down steadies your hand.

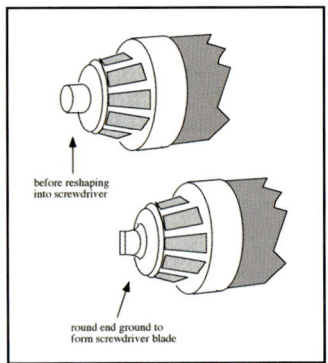

Figure 10-F

- To mount a disc or a wheel onto a screw-mount mandrel, follow these steps: Mount the mandrel on your handpiece, put the screw through the hole in the disc to be mounted, insert the tip of the screw into the mandrel, press it with your thumb, and gently depress the foot pedal. The disc quickly mounts itself, requiring just a little tightening with the small screwdriver. To easily accomplish this last step, keep a screwdriver in a hole in your bench top that is parallel with your bench pin. (Only the handle of the screwdriver is visible; the rest is sheathed in the bench.) As an alternative, you can grind the round stub on the Chuck key into a screwdriver shape (Figure 10-F), creating a combination Chuck key and screwdriver tool.

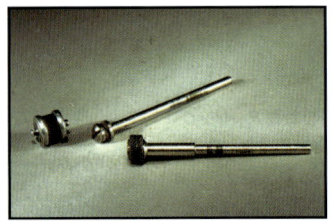

Figure 10-G

- The flint wheel from an older-style disposable lighter makes a great carbide steel bur. Find an empty lighter, knock and pry apart the fly wheel, and place it on a screw mandrel (Figure 10-G). You've now got a carbide bur that works like a rotary file for filing edges and removing coarse metal.

Bottled Up: Creating a Safety Shield

Bradney Simon of Bench Media in Spartanburg, South Carolina, offers the following tip to help prevent polishing compound from being thrown back into your face: a plastic shield that slips over the flex-shaft handpiece.

To make the shield, take a plastic water bottle and cut off the bottom. Leaving the neck of the bottle intact, cut away one side. Slip the bottle neck-first over the flex-shaft. Heat the bottle neck gently, pressing it against the flex-shaft and re-shaping the softened plastic for a snug fit against the handpiece. (To avoid burning your fingers during this step, use a towel to hold the hot plastic.) Allow the plastic to cool.

The finished shield can be slipped on and off the flex-shaft, depending on the types of tools you're using. Because the plastic is clear, you can see your work through the shield. And if it gets scratched or otherwise damaged, plastic bottles are cheap enough that you can build as many shields as needed.

Of Mops & Magnets

Keeping your bench organized can be easier than you think. Mop or broom wall clips, for instance, can hold handpieces that aren't in use, suggests designer Frank Goss of Houston. In addition, magnets can keep burs close at hand. "I use a magnet screwed to the bench face to hold the three or four burs that I might be using for a given setting," Goss explains. "That way I don't have to keep placing them in the bur carousel and hunting for them when I need them, or searching for them in the pan. When I'm done, I replace them in the carousel."

The Every-Stylish Flat Top Bur

Figure 10-H

Arthur Anton Skuratowicz of Anton Nash in Colorado Springs, Colorado, offers the following tip to rejuvenate old burs: "Even re-sharpened burs will ultimately wear out, but you can give them new life by grinding their tips and exposing a new cutting edge (Figure 10-H). This modification can be performed on any bur—setting, hart, even ball burs—and the resulting surface works well for tight spots where you need a safety edge, such as the inside of a bezel. By further polishing the flat area, you can ensure the tool has less friction and offers greater control.

"I first tried this trick when I needed a bur to clean out a groove for inlaying opal; later, I found my new tool worked well for many other applications—cleaning solder from the inside of a flat-back bezel, adjusting prong seats on large settings, and carving wax. In this case, a flat top will never go out of style."

Jewelers' Resources

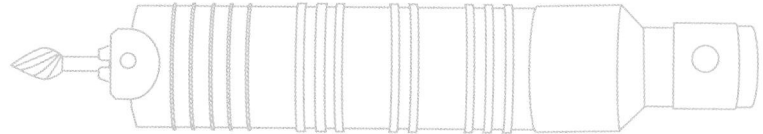

Resource Index

Rio Grande	81
3M Inc.	82
The Foredom Electric Co.	83
MJSA/AJM Press	84
The Ganoksin Project	85
Ruehle-Diebener-Publishing Co.	86
Indian Jewelers Supply Co.	87
Metalwerx	88
Manufacturing Jewelers & Suppliers of America	89
Otto Frei	90
RaceCar Jewelry	91
Revere Academy of Jewelry Arts	92
Ti-Research	93

A Winning Combination for Jewelry Flex-shafts

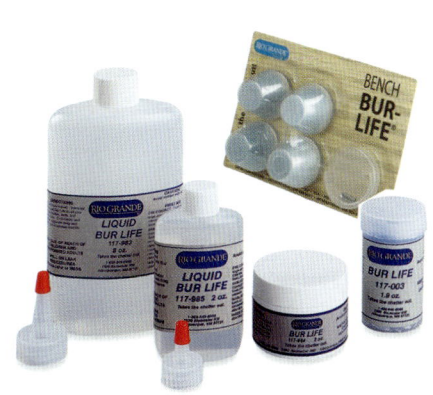

To most bench jewelers, the flex-shaft is a frequently used and indispensable tool in their studio. Many have discovered that the burs they use and the way they use them can significantly improve their flex-shaft's performance as well as their final results—whether they're cutting, stone-setting or finishing. To get the most out of their flex-shafts, jewelers rely on two products designed to provide maximum efficiency: LYNX™ burs and Bur-Life® tool lubricant.

LYNX™ burs, by Hager & Meisinger, are recognized throughout the world for their high quality, smooth cutting action and long life. Manufactured to extremely close tolerances, these burs cut metal without the "chatter" or "grabbing" that can occur with some lesser-quality burs—the cuts you get from LYNX burs are smoother, easier and more uniform. And, because they are made from a tungsten vanadium alloy, they retain their sharpness over time and through long use. Many sizes and styles are available, including round, cup, concave and stone-setting.

Bur-Life® lubricant significantly reduces friction to give burs a smoother cutting action, more control and a longer life. Unlike other lubricants that are repelled by heat, Bur-Life's formula is actually attracted to heat, so it is drawn right to the point of the bur's contact with the metal, adding lubrication where it's needed most. The result is a better finish on your pieces, faster working time and burs that last and last. Bur-Life can also be used with files, saw blades, gravers and other tools.

LYNX™ burs and Bur-Life® are both offered exclusively from Rio Grande through the *Tools & Equipment* catalog.

RIO GRANDE® Since 1944

7500 Bluewater NW, Albuquerque, NM 87121
Phone: 800-545-6566 • Fax: 800-965-2329
info@riogrande.com • www.riogrande.com

3M™ FX Polishing Wheel

A Conformable Wheel for Finishing Precious Metals

The FX Polishing Wheel features a consistent premium grade of silicon carbide mineral along with brightness enhancers that result in controllable, consistent finishing and polishing of metal parts. This new molded wheel technology can apply semi- and final finishes on platinum, titanium, precious metal clay, brass, cobalt, and chrome.

Conformable Polishing

The FX Polishing Wheel uses a conformable resin system, which results in a wheel that can follow contours, curves, and unique part geometries.

Uniform Finish, Part After Part

The FX Polishing Wheel can remove surface defects, blend surface finishes, and enhance and polish metal parts to a uniform, consistent finish. And that finish is controllable—as the wheel is being used, the same grade of mineral with brightness enhancers keep coming to the surface to do the work, providing you with a consistent finish, part after part.

Fewer Rejects and Less Clean-up Saves Money

The FX Polishing Wheel can be dressed and shaped using coated abrasives or dressing tools. The result is a user-friendly polishing wheel that has a reduced tendency to create rejects and rework, which translates to increased production yields. Using the FX Polishing Wheel with Trizact™ abrasives or 3M Bristle™ products can reduce or possibly eliminate buffing operations, which is less processing time and clean-up while producing a more consistent finish.

Size: 4" X 1" X 1" Max RPM 3,600	
Product	**UPC**
FX M S 240	048011-33720
FX M S 320	048011-33721
FX M S 600	048011-33722
FX M S 800	048011-33725
FX M S 1500	048011-33726
FX M S 3000	048011-33727

3M

Customer Response Center
900 Bush Ave., Building 21-1W-10
St. Paul, MN 55106
Phone: 1-866-279-1288, ext. 1225
www.3M.com/creativearts

The Leader in Flex-Shaft Tools

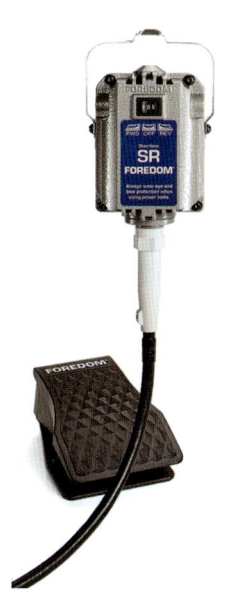

Our all new ⅙ horsepower Series SR combines the best features of our most popular motors—power, dependability, reversibility—into one more powerful model. Its introduction is another example of Foredom innovation and why Foredom continues to be your best choice in flex shaft power tools.

Foredom power tools and accessories are used worldwide by professional bench jewelers and in many others working industrial, craft, art, and lab applications. With models ranging in horsepower from ⅒ to ⅓, foot and dial speed controls, and 21 handpieces to choose from there is sure to be one suitable for your application.

Since 1922, Foredom has manufactured flexible shaft power tools and is still the leader today. Foredom manufactures the largest selection of quality motors, speed controls, and handpieces and offers the most comprehensive assortment of rotary power tool accessories to use with them. As the industry leader our flex-shafts are often copied but never equaled.

Foredom manufactures other equipment for professional jewelers and technicians including the BL lathe. This compact, bench top model features variable speed up to 7,000 rpm for polishing, sanding, cleaning, texturing and other finishing applications on metals, plastics, and wood.

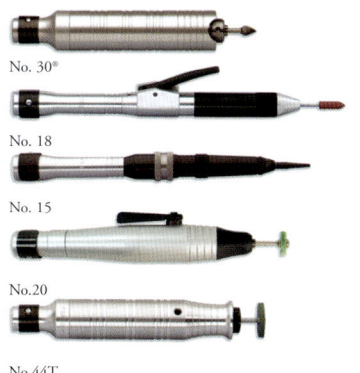

No. 30®
No. 18
No. 15
No. 20
No. 44T

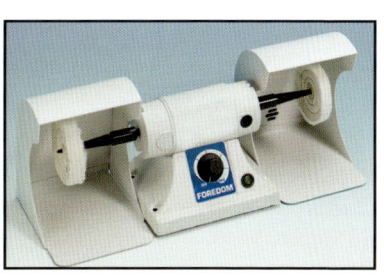

FOREDOM®

The Foredom Electric Company
16 Stony Hill Road • Bethel, CT 06801
Tel.:203-792-8622 • Fax: 203-796-7861
info@foredom.com • www.foredom.com

101 Bench Tips for Jewelers
Learn Alan Revere's Most Valuable Tricks

Acclaimed as a designer, author, educator, and innovator, Alan Revere shares his most valuable bench tips and tricks in *101 Bench Tips for Jewelers*. Published by MJSA/AJM Press and based on Alan's monthly column in *AJM* Magazine, this book will help any jeweler speed production, improve quality, and raise profits at the bench.

It covers all aspects of bench work—from soldering to stone setting, piercing to final polish—with full-color illustrations by Sean Kane depicting each tip in exacting detail. Discover how you can easily modify common bench tools to enhance productivity, and how household items such as dental floss and paper clips can become valuable bench aids. See why this book won the Gold Excel Award from the Society of National Association Publications.

A division of Manufacturing Jewelers & Suppliers of America (MJSA), MJSA/AJM Press publishes books on all aspects of making and selling jewelry. Many of its titles are based on articles that have appeared in MJSA's flagship monthly magazine, *AJM: The Authority on Jewelry Manufacturing*. These titles include:

- *The Platinum Bench* by Jurgen Maerz
- *At the Bench* by Gregg Todd and Greg Gilman
- *The* AJM *Guide to Lost-Wax Casting*
- *Working with Gemstones: A Bench Jeweler's Guide* by Arthur Skuratowicz and Julie Nash
- *The* AJM *Handbook on Best Business Practices*

For more information about any MJSA/AJM Press book, visit MJSA Online at *www.mjsainc.com*.

45 Royal Little Drive
Providence, RI 02904
1-800-444-6572 • Fax 1-401-274-0265
E-mail: *mjsa@mjsainc.com*
www.mjsainc.com

The Ganoksin Project
Your Online Information Resource

The Ganoksin Project hosts the largest single virtual information source for searchable archived content for jewelry and metals in the world. It has an impressive library of thousands of articles, reports, and technical data on gem and jewelry-related topics, as well as a sizable collection of art and jewelry galleries, for both the casual visitor and the professional—ALL OPEN TO THE PUBLIC AND FREE OF CHARGE! It is now the largest compilation of Web-accessible jewelry-related information in the world. The Ganoksin Project also hosts the popular online discussion forum for jewelers called Orchid.

Orchid's 6,200 members foster sharing, support community, enhance productivity, and encourage studio safety by promoting education in the jewelry and metal arts worldwide. Orchid is both a reservoir of content and a network of active relationships for the benefit of the gem and jewelry industries.

Orchid is a place to make friends, to hear diverse opinions, and debate. Orchid provides a platform to facilitate business, to build trust as well as bridges between race, age, gender, culture, experience, and levels of socioeconomic status. Orchid provides a path that leads to a road of shared exploring, learning, and creativity.

With list members from all over the world, speaking from a wide range of technical and aesthetic experiences, this lively forum addresses questions about every aspect of jewelry making today.

We invite you to explore and discover what thousands of other jewelers, gem dealers, and metals enthusiasts have. Go to *http://www.ganoksin.com*.

The Ganoksin Project
Bangkok, Thailand
service@ganoksin.com
www.ganoksin.com

Practical Goldsmith Series

Everyday life often prevents the natural desire among goldsmiths to be comprehensively informed of the latest state of the art technology in jewelry production. Specialist information must first be researched and reference books often appear outdated.

The "Practical Goldsmith" offers new impulses, which have now been published as a manual with a series of courses. In a contemporary and clear form, it presents current products and instruments to do with the entire range of studio processes in goldsmith art and jewelry production. The specialist compendium addresses young professionals as an aid in getting started and also jewelry professionals to enhance their knowledge and provide information.

Fundamental goldsmith techniques are presented in exercises covering the first steps to the finish in handling precious metals. Goldsmiths will find in the series' modern tools and resources for the studio and the drawing board in goldsmith studios.

- Practical Platinumsmith 1
  All on platinum working
- Practical Goldsmith 2
  Modelling and Moulding
- Practical Goldsmith 3
  Mounting - Settings
- Practical Goldsmith 4
  Mounting – Joints - Electroplating
- Practical Goldsmith 5
  Mounting - Clasps
- Practical Goldsmith 6
  Palladium
- Practical Goldsmith 7
  Silver Part 1
- Practical Goldsmith 8
  Silver Part 2
- Practical Goldsmith 9
  New techniques and auxiliaries
- Practical Goldsmith 10
  New techniques
- Practical Goldsmith 11
  ColorIt Design
- Practical Goldsmith 12
  Chasing + Inlay work
- Practical Goldsmith 13
  Granulation + Niello Work

Ruehle-Diebener-Publishing Co.

Industriestr. 4, D- 70565 Stuttgart / Germany

T: ++49 711 976670 F: ++49 711 9766749

rdv@gz-online.com

www.gz-journal.de/welcome.cfm

Flexshafts & Much More

From humble beginnings in 1943, I.J.S. grew by offering its clients quality, selection, and competitive price. While jewelers are the bulk of our clientele, we serve a diverse group of skilled craftsmen, including makers of trophy buckles and horse tack, musical instruments, knives, swords, pow-wow regalia, and sculptures.

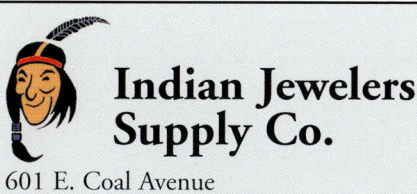

Indian Jewelers Supply Co.

601 E. Coal Avenue
Gallup, NM 87301-6005
ph 1-505-722-4451 or 1-800-545-6940
fax 1-505-722-4172 or 1-888-722-4172

2105 San Mateo Boulevard NE
Albuquerque, NM 87110
ph 1-505-265-3701   fax 1-505-266-5548

www.ijsinc.com

Our offerings include:

- Flexshaft motors and controls by Foredom® and GrobetUSA®.
- Rotary and impact handpieces by Foredom® and MagnaGraver®.
- Accessories for cutting, grinding, sanding, polishing, and stonesetting.
- Gemstones: faceted, cabochons, beads, and rough.
- Metals: Sterling/Fine Silver, Karat Golds, Silver- and Goldfilled, Copper, Nickel, Brasses and Bronzes. Sheets, Wires, Discs/Ovals, Casting Grains, and Solders.
- Tools for casting, fabrication, soldering/brazing, lapidary, engraving, and finishing.
- Showroom displays and packaging.

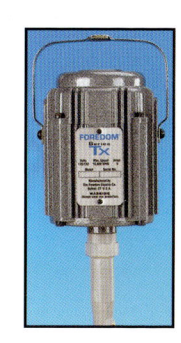

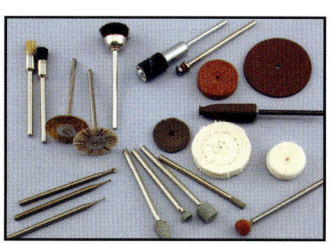

Metalwerx: Expert Instruction with a Personal Touch

Established in 1998 and located in Waltham, Massachusetts, Metalwerx offers intensive instruction for the novice and the professional. With our fully equipped studio, your learning experience at Metalwerx is one that you will remember. If you are a bench jeweler looking to hone your skills or a metals enthusiast learning to make jewelry for the first time, Metalwerx has something for you. We offer small, personable classes with a community feel.

Technical Workshops

If you are thinking about a profession in jewelry, currently attend a bench jewelers program, or work in a jewelry store, we have 2-5 day workshops that will help you hone your skills. Workshops in mechanisms, pavé stone setting, or classical chain-making and granulation are part of our curriculum. Innovation is at the forefront of our class structure, allowing for workshops in the latest techniques with the flexible shaft or hydraulic press.

Art in Metals

Our workshops also reflect Metalwerx's commitment to the metal arts. Classes such as "Found Objects," "Resin Inlay," "Weaving with Wire," and "Art of the Tin Can" explore our innate need to embellish.

Metalwerx Community

Metalwerx is home to 15 studiomates – a group of passionate amateurs, bench jewelers, and professionals who form a vibrant and active community. Studiomates enjoy 24-hour access within a dedicated 1500 square foot area of the building. Each studiomate has his or her own workspace, shares a soldering and polishing area, a computer with Internet access, specialty tools, kilns, a rolling mill, and the library.

Metalwerx
50 Guinan St. • Waltham, MA 02451
Phone: 781 891 3854 • Fax: 781 891 3857
www.metalwerx.com

MJSA Offers Jewelers Resources to Succeed

For successful bench repair and fabrication, jewelers must have both the right techniques and the right tools. Through Manufacturing Jewelers & Suppliers of America's publications, trade shows, and educational programs, they're able to find both.

MJSA's flagship trade show, **Expo New York**, is the largest trade show dedicated to jewelry manufacturing. Each year, nearly 6,000 buyers attend Expo to find the latest manufacturing equipment, the widest array of tools and supplies, and the latest technical information.

MJSA's monthly magazine, **AJM: The Authority on Jewelry Manufacturing**, offers a wealth of technical and business expertise for companies of all sizes. Those offerings include an "At the Bench" section featuring step-by-step projects for gold, silver, and platinum, as well as invaluable tips by such leading goldsmiths as Alan Revere, Charles Lewton-Brain, and Jurgen Maerz.

The **MJSA Jewelry Academy** provides quality training by industry professionals, with classes offered nationwide. Technical courses offer a combination of classroom instruction and hands-on experience. Courses include stone setting, soldering, electroplating, bench assembly, CAD/CAM, and more.

Members of MJSA receive discounts on all of these resources, as well as exclusive referrals to potential customers and cost-saving benefits. To find out more about why it pays to be an MJSA member, contact the association at 1-401-274-3840, e-mail *mjsa@mjsainc.com*, or visit *www.mjsainc.com*.

45 Royal Little Drive
Providence, RI 02904
1-800-444-6572 • Fax 1-401-274-0265
E-mail: *mjsa@mjsainc.com*
www.mjsainc.com

Think Otto Frei
For Flex-shaft Sales and Service

Otto Frei has a service department that can repair your old flex-shaft handpiece. Give us a call or e-mail us at service@ottofrei.com to find out if parts are still available for your handpiece and to discuss whether or not it is worth repairing.

We are the prime source for parts for the Swiss-made Technique, the older Swedish-made Techno, and the Swiss-made Badeco handpieces. Visit our Web site for parts lists and great deals on handpieces, flex-shafts, and over 20,000 tools and findings, all with current pricing and availability.

See our Web site for special Internet-only pricing on all the latest flex-shaft kits.

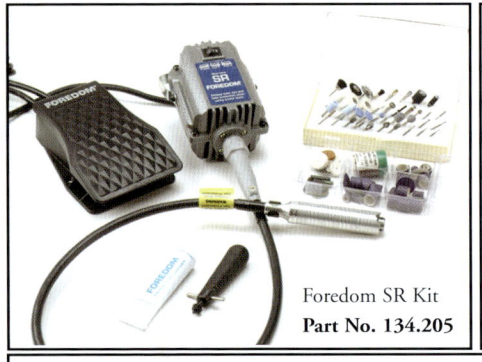

Foredom SR Kit
Part No. 134.205

Ottoflex Swiss Made Technique Kit
Part No. 134.217

Badeco Swiss Hammer Handpiece
Part No. 134.751

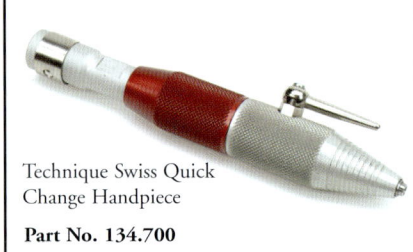

Technique Swiss Quick Change Handpiece
Part No. 134.700

Otto Frei
Quality Jewelry Tools & Findings Since 1930

Phone: 1-800-772-3456 • 1-510-832-0355
Fax: 1-800-900-3734 • 1-510-834-6217
ottofrei.com

What Can RaceCar Jewelry Do for You?

If you make your items by hand, you may get to the point where you no longer have the time to do everything yourself. That's when you need to talk with a manufacturer who can explain all the ins and outs of having your designs turned into a reality. You need a company that's able to advise you on how to make the original model, or that can make the model from your designs. You need a company that can produce your models strictly for you, to exacting specifications.

You need RaceCar Jewelry.

We work in a variety of metals, including:
14k yellow • 14k white • 14k green • 14k rose • 18k yellow • 18k white • 18k green • 18k rose • 22k yellow • gold alloys for enamellists • brass, bronze, and white bronze • pewter and white metal • sterling deox silver • pure silver.

We also perform the following processes:
Mold making • model making • CAD/CAM • CNC milling • hand polishing and finishing • soldering (of findings) • fusion welding and assembly • gold and rhodium plating (for items we produce) • two-part epoxy/enameling.

So whether you're a designer or jeweler, own a store or operate out of a one-person shop, RaceCar Jewelry will produce your designs the way you want them—and allow you the freedom, time, and energy to develop new designs and market your creations.

RaceCar Jewelry Co. Inc.
52 Glen Road • Cranston, RI 02920
1-401-461-7870 • Fax: 401-270-1196
sales@racecarjewelry.com • www.racecarjewelry.com

Revere Academy of Jewelry Arts
The School of Jewelry Professionals

"Gold has its value, but learning is priceless." — **Ancient Chinese Proverb**

Since 1979, thousands of bench jewelers and jewelry designers, serious hobbyists and career-bound beginners have come from around the world to attend the Revere Academy. Our classes are taught at a professional level in the finest studios with top-notch equipment. The most common comments we hear from students are, "I can't believe I learned so much in such a short time," and "I wish I had done this years ago."

Don't wait. Learn skills today that you can use tomorrow and for years to come. Revere classes are taught by working professionals who demonstrate the skills they use every day. Select a program that meets your needs and schedule, from a single one-day specialized class to extended diploma programs covering a wide range of subjects.

Our programs include:

- Jewelry Technician Diploma Program
- Graduate Jeweler Diploma Program
- Annual Masters Symposium in April
- JA Certification

Classes:

Anticlastic Raising • Bench Tips • Basic Stone Setting • Casting • Chain Making Channel Setting • Chasing/Repoussé • Design • Enameling • Fabrication • Gemology Gold Soldering • Hand Engraving • Hinges/Mechanisms • Keum-boo • Marketing Metalsmithing • Mold Making • Polishing/Finishing • Rendering • Repair • Pavé Setting Platinum • Prong Setting • Trade Practices • Wax Modeling

For more information, including a free video tour, visit our Web site: revereacademy.com.

Revere Academy of Jewelry Arts
760 Market Street, Suite 900
San Francisco, CA 94102
1-415-391-4179
revereacademy.com

Casting Equipment, Tools, and Know-how for Designers

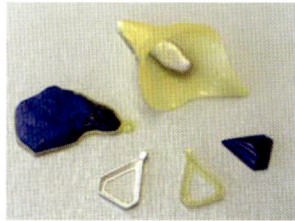

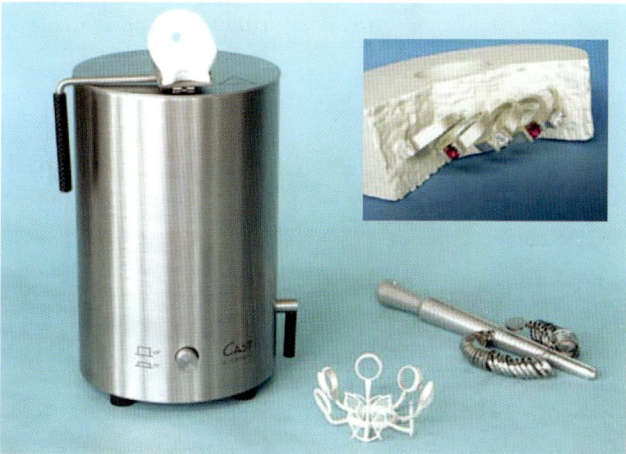

Focused on the requirement of bench jewelers and designers, Ti-Research offers small but highly reliable casting equipment for even the smallest locations.

Measuring about 10 inches high and 6.6 inches in diameter, the compact centrifigal casting machine Cast is an alternative for designers and professional bench jewelers. It eliminates the hassle of sending molds back and forth, losing precious time and expenses for work that can be done in-house.

The smallest unit allows casting of all metals, which can be melted by flame under atmospheric conditions without contamination.

Up to 250 grams of gold or equivalent amounts of other metals can be cast in one cycle. The sprueing is done radially onto the wax disk to most effectively fill the mold during casting; this cuts metal waste by about 50 percent over traditional casting tree methods.

Besides equipment for casting and product-specific supplies, Ti-Research also produces investments for metals with high melting temperatures, such as platinum, as well as reactive metals such as titanium. A common feature of these investments is the short burnout cycle, cutting down the time from sprueing to devesting to two hours.

With the introduction of NoWax, Ti-Research provides a new degree of freedom to designers creating jewelery.

NoWax is a unique new resin compound that can be easily modeled by hand to make jewelry patterns for lost-wax casting. The patterns become hard after light curing and can be filed, drilled, or machined.

Setting of irregular stones or other free-form designs is made easy with NoWax.

The cure process can be easily monitored because NoWax changes color from pink to yellow as it cures, making the work independent from a specific light source. After curing, the patterns are ready to be sprued, just like regular waxes for casting.

To get familiar with the properties of NoWax, designers can purchase a Start-up Kit.

Ti-Reasearch products are available in the U.S. at selected suppliers.

Ti-Research GBR
Am Oberen Buhl 13
D 97350 Mainbernheim Germany
T: ++49 9323 80159 F: ++49 9323 80156
info@ti-research.com
www.ti-research.com

Index to Chapters 1-10

3M EXL wheels, 47
3M Flexible Diamond abrasive, 52
3M Micro-finishing Film, 47, 51
3M Purple Ceramic bands and discs, 46
3M Scotch-Brite Radial Bristle Disc, 45, 47, 50, 53
3M Trizact abrasive, 56
3M Unitized Wheel, 54
3M Wetordry polishing paper, 49

Abrasives
    Aluminum oxide, 45, 47, 49, 50, 51, 52, 54, 55
    Ceramic, 46, 56
    Diamond, 46, 52-53, 55
    Rubberized, 47, 55
    Silicon carbide, 45, 47, 49, 51, 53, 54
    Wax/tallow, 46

AdvantEdge, 47, 55
AJM: The Authority on Jewelry Manufacturing, 73
AllSet System, 64
Aluminum oxide abrasives, 45, 47, 49, 50, 51, 52, 54, 55
Amps, 16, 17, 18
Armature, 11, 12, 68
Ball bur, 30
Bearing bur, 31
Bi-directional Motors, 18
Bobbing compound, 58, 60, 61
Brightboy, 47
Bristle brush, 57, 58
Brush holders, 11
Bud bur, 31, 32
Buff, chamois, 60
Buff, felt, 60
Buff, stitched, 59
Buff, unstitched, 59

Burs
    Ball, 30
    Bearing, 31
    Bud, 31, 32
    Cone, 32

    Cup, 33
    Cross-cut Cylinder, 35
    Cylinder, 35
    Flame, 32
    Florentine, 36
    Hart, 31
    Inverted cone, 32, 33
    Krause, 34
    Setting, 30
    Slim reamer, 33
    Wax bur, 35
    Wheel bur, 34

Bur alloys, 36, 37, 38, 39
Bur lubrication, 36
Carbon brush (for motor), 11, 12, 68
Ceramic abrasives, 46, 56
Collet handpieces, 24, 25, 41
Commutator, 11, 12
Compressed fiber wheel, 54
Cone bur, 32
Cratex, 47, 55
Cross-cut cylinder bur, 35
Cup bur, 33
Cut-off wheel, 54
Cylinder bur, 35
Dial control rheostat, 14, 20
Diamond abrasives, 46, 52, 53, 55
Disc mandrel, 42
Drill bit, 27, 28, 29, 37, 38, 39
Drill press, 63
Drum arbor, 43
Duplex spring assembly, 23, 24
Edenta, 47, 55
Field (magnetic), 11, 12
Fisher, John, 62
Flame bur, 32
Florentine bur, 36
Foot pedal, 14, 19
Foredom CW wheel, 46

The Ganoksin Project, 73
Goss, Frank, 77
Gray Star compound, 61
Hammering ("hammer") handpiece, 24, 25
Handpiece holder, 65
Handpiece attachment to shaft, 13, 26
Hart bur, 31
Heatless wheels, 53
Horsepower, 16, 18
Inverted cone bur, 32, 33
Jacobs, Arthur Irving, 21
Jacobs Chuck handpiece, 13, 21, 22, 24, 25, 41, 63
Jacobs Chuck key, 22
Jump ring cutting jig, 63
Jump Ringer, 63
Krause bur, 34
Lewton-Brain, Charles, 71, 72, 76
Maintenance procedures, 67-69
Mandrels
    Disc, 42
    Drum arbor, 43
    Polishing point, 44
    Screw, 41
    Snap-on, 42
    Split, 43, 52
    Standard, 41
    Tapered (spiral), 44
Manufacturing Jewelers & Suppliers of America (MJSA), 73
Matt Bracelet Shaper, 65
Matt wax lathe, 65
Matt Wax Trimmer, 65
Maudslay, Henry, 9, 10
MetalMaster, 47
Milling table, 64
"Mizzy" wheels, 53
Moore's disc, 51
Motor Shaft, 11
Nasmyth, James Hall, 9, 10
Ohms, 17
Permanent magnet motors, 17
Permanently mounted accessories, 42

Polishing compounds, 46, 52, 60-62
Polishing point mandrel, 44
Porcelain polishing tips, 56
Pumice, 55, 56
Quick-release handpiece, 13, 22, 23, 25
Rouge, 59, 61, 62
RPM, 16, 18
Rubberized abrasives, 47, 55
Safety procedures, 71, 72
Sanding disc, 51
Sandpaper, 48
Screw mandrel, 41
Separating disc, 54
Setting bur, 30
Silicon carbide abrasives, 45, 47, 49, 51, 53, 54, 55
Simon, Brad, 77
Skuratowicz, Arthur Anton, 78
Slim reamer, 33
Snap-on disc, 51
Snap-on mandrel, 42, 51
Spade bit, 28, 29
Split mandrel, 43, 52
Standard mandrel, 41
Tapered (spiral) mandrel, 44
Texturing wheel, 58
Tripoli, 59, 60, 61
Tube setting, 73-75
Universal motor, 17
Volts, 16, 17, 18
Wax bur, 35
Wax/tallow abrasives, 46
Wheel bur, 34
White Diamond compound, 59, 61, 62
Wire brush, 58
Wolf belt sander, 65

About the Author

Karen Christians is the founder and executive director of Metalwerx, Waltham, Massachusetts. Metalwerx is a unique combination of a jewelry and metal arts school and a fifteen-member community studio. In 1998, she began contributing to Ganoksin's Orchid Forum, where she is still active. Karen obtained her BFA with High Honors from the Massachusetts College of Art in Boston, Massachusetts. She enjoys traveling and meeting other goldsmiths in different countries.